SOME REMINISCENCES

(1838–1918)

BY

COLONEL H. W. WILLIAMS, D.L., J.P.

PENZANCE

J. A. D. BRIDGER

NEW AND SECOND-HAND BOOKSELLER, PUBLISHER, ETC.

112A AND 112B MARKET JEW STREET

1918

TO ONE

WHO HAS

FOR MORE THAN FIFTY YEARS

BEEN MY

DEVOTED COMPANION AND DEAREST FRIEND

MY BELOVED WIFE

INTRODUCTION

I AM introducing these Recollections, at the special request of numerous friends.

In doing so I wish distinctly to point out that I make no claim to any literary merit.

In the course of an extremely busy life, I have had no opportunity to become an accomplished writer.

I have endeavoured in very simple language to record those instances in which I have been more or less interested, including various conversations which have taken place in my numerous railway journeys. It was my original intention to print only a few copies for personal friends, but by urgent request I have decided to publish them in the ordinary way.

H. W. WILLIAMS.

St. Ives, Cornwall,
Easter, 1918.

CONTENTS

SOME REMINISCENCES

(1838–1918)

CHAPTER I

HAVING been blessed with a long life and a very retentive memory, and having held for many years various important positions, I have been requested to place on record some of my early recollections.

Having never kept a diary, I am fully aware there will be many omissions and commissions.

I may at once say that I have lived under four reigns, and am therefore able to refer back for almost eighty years. I distinctly remember as a child seeing at St. Ives a display of fireworks, at the Coronation of Queen Victoria on June 28th, 1838.

I was born at St. Ives, Cornwall, on the 23rd July, 1834.

My father, Thomas Williams, as a lad at sea was taken prisoner of war by a French Privateer, and I think I cannot do better than insert the following extract from his Journal, which is interesting, as it gives full particulars of his capture, trial, and pardon.

THE ADVENTURES OF THOMAS WILLIAMS,

OF ST. IVES, CORNWALL,

PRISONER OF WAR IN FRANCE
FROM MARCH, 1804, TO MAY, 1814.

[EXTRACT FROM DIARY.]

" I was taken prisoner of war by the French on the 28th day of March, 1804, on board the brig *Friendship*, of London, Josias Sincock, master, coming from London laden with copper and flour for Devonport Dockyard, and having weighed anchor in the Downs, and sailing down the Channel with a fair wind under convoy of the *Spider* gun-brig, and we not being a fast sailer, and also having being detained too long in the Downs to take on board a new long-boat, we were much astern of the fleet when night came on. About 6 o'clock in the evening I was on the forecastle looking out when we espied a lugger coming towards the shore upon a wind and went into land ahead of us, and close under the stern of an East Indiaman, who was then reefing topsails. We lost sight of the lugger for some time. At length we espied her coming up close astern of us. We hailed her, but got no reply. At length she shear'd up under our quarter, and hove a grapnel on board, and very soon a great number of the crew came on board well arm'd, and took possession of our ship, drove all the ship's company below, and kept sentry over the hatchways. But I was ordered on deck to shew them where the leading ropes were. They soon altered our course for the coast of France, the lugger keeping us company the whole night. In the morning early we were close into Dieppe, not having seen an English cruiser during the whole time. When the tide suited we were put into the harbour, and the same night put on shore into a round tower, and there kept for three days. Before we landed they took away all our clothes, except what we had on, and they had the audacity to come to see us in prison with our men's clothes on them. We began our march towards Givet and Charlémont in the Province of Ardennes on the 1st day of April, and we were a fortnight in getting to our journey's end, being lodged in filthy prisons at night, and with a guard by day, having travelled nearly 300 miles on a pound of brown bread. When we arrived at Givet prison we found several other ships' companies there before us."

The subjoined is a copy of the curious judgment and pardon :—

JUDGMENT

Judgment rendered by the Military Commission formed at Givet in execution of the Imperial Decree of the 17th of Frimaire in the 14th year of the Republic.

For and by the Emperor of the French, King of Italy, Protector of the Confederation of the Rhine, Mediator of the Swiss Confederation, etc., etc.

This sixteenth day of March, one thousand eight hundred and eleven. The Military Commission formed by virtue of the Imperial Decree of the 17th of Frimaire in the 14th year composed conformably to this Decree of Messieurs—

Fonton, Chief of the Battalion, sous Director of Artillery, Member of the Legion of Honour, President.

Hubert, Captain of the 34th Regiment of Infantry, Member of the Legion of Honour.

Peyren, Captain of the 34th Regiment of Infantry and Member of the Legion of Honour.

Navarre, Captain of the 34th Regiment of Infantry; and Sainton, Captain Quartermaster of 34th Regiment of Infantry, Member of the Legion of Honour.

M. Dontor, Member of the Legion of Honour, Lieutenant of the Imperial Gendarmerie of the Department of Mont Tonnerre, doing the functions of reporter and Imperial Procurer. All nominated by Monsieur Lascoste, General of the Division, one of the Commanders of the Legion of Honour, Commanding in Chief the Second Military Territorial Division; assisted by Gamant, Horse Brigadier of the Imperial Gendarmerie of the Department of the Ardennes, Register appointed by the Reporter; and Howlet, Prisoner of War, who was sworn to accomplish his charge faithfully.

The above mentioned, according to the terms of the 7th and 8th Articles of the Law of the 13th Brumaire, in the 3rd year of the Republic, are not related nor allied neither of them nor prevented in the Decree prohibited by the Constitution.

The Commission convocated by the order of Monsieur Ledee, General of Brigade, Officer of the Legion of Honour, Commander at Arms of the places of Charlemount and Givet, assembled in the grand hall of the hotel of these towns, in order to judge—

1st. Henry Blight, age 30 years, gunner of the *Recovery* privateer, native of Ludgvan, County of Cornwall, in England, 1 metre 71 centimetres high, light brown hair and eyebrows, blue eyes, full-coloured face, ordinary nose and chin, middling mouth.

2nd. Thomas Williams, aged 24 years, apprentice on board the merchant ship *Friendship*, a native of St. Ives, County of Cornwall, England, 1 metre 62 centimetres high, hair and eyebrows chestnut colour, full coloured face, lightly mark'd with the small-pox, slight nose, dimpled chin, and middling mouth.

3rd. Robert Burn, aged 19 years, apprentice on board the merchant ship *Blenheim*, a native of Beverley, in Yorkshire, England, 1 metre 69 centimetres high, hair and eyebrows dark brown, blue eyes, full coloured face, lightly mark'd with the small-pox, pointed nose, round chin, middling mouth.

All three prisoners of war, detained in the depôt of Givet.

The Sessions being opened, the president caused to be brought and placed before him by the Register on the Bureau, an exemplary of the Laws of the 9th of Prairial, in the 3rd year, and of the 13th of Brumaire, in the 5th year, and of the Imperial Decree of the 17th of Frimaire, in the 14th year, and afterwards demanded of the Reporter the Lecture of the Report of the verbal process of Information and generally all the people as well for the defence of as against the accused to the number of five.

This lecture being finished, the president ordered the guards to bring forth the prisoners, who were introduced free and without irons before the Commission. The accused persons on being asked their names, age, profession, place of birth, and rank, answered :—

1st. Henry Blight, age 30 years, gunner, native of Ludgvan, County of Cornwall, in England, prisoner of war of the depôt of Givet. 2nd. Thomas

Williams, age 24 years, apprentice, native of
St. Ives, County of Cornwall, in England, prisoner
of war of the depôt of Givet. 3rd. Robert Burn,
age 19 years, apprentice, native of Beverley, in
Yorkshire, England, prisoner of war of the depôt of
Givet.

After having made known to accused the facts
laid to their charge, and caused them to be
interrogated separately by the organ of the
president, who heard the Reporter in his report
and conclusions, and the accused in the means of
their defence as well by those as by their official
defender, who, having declared that they had
nothing more to add in their defence, then the
President asked the members of the Commission
if they had any observations to make, to which
they answered in the negative, and before he called
the votes, ordered the defender and the accused
to retire. The latter were reconducted by their
escort to the town prison. The register and the
citizens withdrew at the request of the president,
the doors being shut and no one present with
the Military Commission but the Reporter and
Imperial Procurer. The president stated the
following questions :—

1st. Henry Blight, as above mentioned, accused
of having deserted. Is he guilty ?
2nd. Thomas Williams, as above mentioned,
accused of having deserted. Is he guilty ?
3rd. Robert Burn, as above mentioned, accused
of having deserted. Is he guilty ?

The votes having been gathered by beginning
with the inferior in and the youngest in each rank,
the president giving his last, the Military Commission unanimously declared that Henry Blight is
guilty, and by the majority of 5 voices to 4 that

Thomas Williams and Robert Burn are guilty; on which the Reporter and Imperial Procurer made their request for the application of the penalty.

The votes, gathered again by the president in the same form as above, the sentence was made public. The Register retook his seat. The president pronounced publicly and with a loud voice the following judgment :—The Military Commission, doing justice to the request of the Reporter and Imperial Procurer, unanimously condemns Henry Blight, and by the majority of 5 voices to 4, Thomas Williams and Robert Burn, prisoners of war, of the depôt of Givet, to suffer six years in irons, and to reimburse all the expenses of the trial, according to the 1st article of the Law of the 9th Prairial, in the 3rd year, and to the Ministerial Letter of the 14th of July, 1807.

Thus : Law of the 9th of Prairial, 3rd year, 1st Article, Any individual made prisoner of war by the armies of the Republic, or detained as such, who without permission from Government shall quit his place of detention or residence, shall suffer six years in irons.

Ministerial Letter of 14th July, 1807.

Every judgment of a Military Commission or of a Permanent Council of War, condemning any person whatever, shall pronounce at the same time that the person condemned shall reimburse to the profit of the public treasure all the expenses of his trial and condemnation. It is likewise ordered that 100 copies of this present judgment shall be printed and distributed. The Reporter is to read the present judgment to the condemned persons in presence of the guard assembled under arms, and to put it in execution immediately.

It is likewise ordered that according to the 39th article of the 13th of Brumaire, in the 5th year, by the president and Reporter, a copy of the present judgment should be sent to His Excellence the Minister of War, and another to the General of the Division. Done, closed and judged at the same sitting in Public Sessions at Givet the same day, month, and year, as above, and the members of the Commission, with the Reporter and Register, have minuted the present judgment.

(Signed) NAVARRE, SAINTON, PEYREN, HABERT, FONTON, President; DONTOR, Reporter; GAMANT, Register.

And the same day the present judgment has been read to the condemned persons in the presence of the guard by the Reporter.

(Signed) . DONTOR.

By a copy confirmed the Register of Military Commission, Gamant; and the Reporter of the Military Commission, Dontor.

PARDON

Napoleon, by the Grace of God and the Constitutions of the Empire, Emperor of the French, King of Italy, Protector of the Confederation of the Rhine, Mediator of the Swiss Confederation, etc., etc., etc.

To the first president, presidents, and counsellors, composing our Imperial Court at Grenoble.— We have received the demand which was made to us in the name of Thomas Williams, English seaman, prisoner of war, condemned by a Military Court Martial, sitting at Givet, dated 16th March, 1811, to the punishment of six years in irons, for having eloped from the depôt of Givet, detained at

Briançon, in order to obtain our pardon, and having observed that divers circumstances might incline us to make him sensible of the effects of the clemency, we have reunited in a Privy Council, in our Palace at St. Cloud, the 4th of August, 1811, our Cousin, the Prince, Arch-Chancellor of the Empire, the Prince Chief of the Departments beyond the Alps, our Cousins Prince Vice-Elector, Prince Vice-Constable ; the Duke of Massa, Great Judge Minister of Justice, and Feltre, Minister of War ; Count Dacres, Minister of Marines ; the Count of Lacepede, Minister of State, President of the Senate ; Count Boulay, President of the Legislative Body ; and Deformon, Minister of State, President of the Section of Finances ; Count Garnier, Senator, the Counsellors of State ; Count Muriare, First President of Court of Abrogation ; Count Merlin, Counsellor of State, our Chief Solicitor in the same Court ; and after having heard the Duke of Massa's report and the advice of the other members of the Council, every thing seen and examined, choosing to prefer mercy to the rigour of the law, we have declared and do declare to forgive the said Thomas Williams fully and entirely.

We command and order that these presents, sealed with the seal of the Empire, be presented to you, by our Chief Solicitor, in the said Court, in public audience, where the offender will be conducted to hear it read, standing, and his head uncovered, in presence of the officers commanding the gendarmerie at Grenoble ; that the said presents be afterwards transcribed on your registers, by the request of the same solicitor, with the annotation of the margin from the minute of pronouncing his condemnation.

Given in our Palace of the Tuileries, under the

B

Seal of the Empire, on the fifteenth day of August, in the year one thousand eight hundred and eleven.

(Signed)　　NAPOLEON.

Seen by us Arch-Chancellors of the Empire.　*　*　*　*　*
By the Emperor,
The Minister Secretary of State.

*　*　*　*

The Great Judge Minister of Justice,
Le Duc de Massa.

———

The last sheet of Mr. William's diary, giving an account of his return to his home and friends, runs thus :—

Wind and weather Do.　All the fleet in sight.
　　Do.　　　　Do.　Looking out hard and sharp for land at 2.30 p.m. saw the land right ahead. Wind now S.E. by E. on our starboard tack. We fetched in about Mousehole Island in the Mount's Bay ; one of the officers on the quarter-deck hail'd a boat to come alongside for him. In doing so several of the men jumped in also, and were conveyed on shore, but our captain would not let anyone leave the ship, as his orders were to put us to Plymouth. We tack'd ship and fetch'd St. Michael's Mount. We then took possession of the ship and *let go the anchor*. The officers did not attempt to stop us. In the night a boat came alongside to enquire if any of their friends were on board. Myself and a few more soon got into the boat as we had not much luggage. We soon landed on the Marazion beach, and from there conducted to nearest Public House, and there treated like lords. As soon as I had taken what was needful for

the journey I started for my dear home, and reached St. Ives about 1 o'clock in the morning on the 10th day of May, 1814 ; to my great joy found my dear old mother alive and well. You may well conjecture the joy she manifested at seeing her only son, who had been absent from her 10 years and 5 months.

In taking a retrospective view of the many and dangerous scenes I have pass'd through in an enemy's country, I have great reason to thank the Almighty for His watchful care over me, for having brought me safe through the various vicissitudes, calamities, difficulties, and distresses which I have been exposed to during my adventures ; and after having travelled upwards of 3000 miles in chains, and in dungeons, and very frequently suffered hunger and thirst, and very badly clothed, many times without shoes, and had to march often in severe weather for more than 20 miles per day in the midst of winter, and yet notwithstanding my unworthiness the Almighty supported me and brought me safe again to my native land in health and strength, both in body and mind, for which I give Him all the praise and all the glory.

The Pardon with the great Napoleon's signature is in my possession.

During my connection with the South Western Railway Company, about which I shall refer to hereafter, I had on one occasion an interview with Lord Palmerston at Broadlands near Romsey, when I showed his Lordship the Pardon. I asked him if it was a good signature ; his answer was, " Oh, yes."

Thomas Williams, my father, died 1862 at the age of seventy-five years.

My early education was certainly of a very primitive nature ; my first school was the St. Ives Wesleyan Day School, long since closed as a day school.

At the age of fifteen I began to think of the future, and my first thought was naturally for the sea, but after a few coasting voyages I gave that up and all idea of a seafaring life.

Eventually I was apprenticed to the firm of J. and W. Richards, drapers, St. Ives, and remained with them till July, 1855.

In those days we never heard much of holidays, or of early closing. We opened at 8 a.m. and closed at 8 p.m., except on Saturdays when we remained open till 11 p.m. On the expiration of my apprenticeship I decided to try London.

In those days the thought of going to London required very grave consideration, in fact it was regarded as a serious matter.

I have heard my father say that in his young days a man who had been to London was looked upon as one of importance.

There was a man who, when asked on his return if he had seen the King, replied, " No, but I saw a man who nearly saw the Duke of York."

In my early days the journey from St. Ives to London was far from easy. The first stage was by bus to Hayle, there joining an old paddle steamer for Bristol. On arriving at that city at a very uncertain time, and after spending the night there, the final stage of the journey was by an early Parliamentary train the following day, shunted frequently at Swindon, Didcot, or Reading for other trains to pass, arriving eventually at Paddington some time in the evening.

I may refer to a very interesting case. By the same steamer from Hayle there was another

Cornish lad, and just before the departure of the steamer his mother not only gave him her blessing, but also told him to be sure and wash the back of his neck, and not to forget to say his prayers.

On his arrival in London, he also sought a situation. In his several calls, one being at a large city warehouse well known to me, he saw the principal partner, who told him he had no vacancy. The lad, to touch the old gentleman's heart, said, " Sir, foxes have holes, etc., etc." The city magnate promptly replied, " Stop, young man, and take an old man's advice, and when you are seeking a situation do not begin by quoting Shakespeare."

I feel positive that the youth of this generation have no idea of the advantages they now enjoy over those of fifty to sixty years ago.

At that time there were very few newspapers, all of which had Government stamps ; even the " West Briton " was 6d., and one had to pay 1d. per hour to read the " Times."

There were no Free Libraries, no Free Education, no council schools, no telegrams, no telephones, and to obtain letters one had to apply at the Post Office window and receive them in the street.

There are still many points of interest I well remember in my early days, such as the services at some of the chapels, where the minister, after giving out the number of the hymn, read two lines of each verse. Under the pulpit was what was called the singing-seat, accommodating generally a full band of musicians. On one occasion a band stopped suddenly ; one said to another, " John, what are you doing ? You don't know Jerusalem from Jericho." In fact he had turned over two leaves of his note-book.

At that time in the Parish Church there was a

barrel organ, which I occasionally manipulated. I do not think we had any regular hymn-books, but we could always fall back on Tate and Brady. Referring to the latter, there is an old story that the late Bishop Wilberforce, accompanied by the Baroness Burdett-Coutts, when driving through the City, passed the warehouse of Messrs. George Harker and Co., " Drysalters." The Baroness asked the Bishop what a Drysalter was ; his answer was, " Tate and Brady."

Many years ago, on a journey from Nottingham to Derby, in the same compartment were a Vicar and a Nonconformist local preacher. In the course of conversation, the latter said to the Vicar, " Well, sir, considering the money spent on your education, you ought to preach good sermons ; but I thank the Lord He has opened my mouth to preach without any education." The Vicar replied, " My friend, I assure you such cases are very rare ; I only remember one, that was in Balaam's time."

One of the most interesting and exciting times of my early days was the pilchard fishery from August to December. At that time there was a number of separate companies, consequently there was very keen competition, and at the sound of the Huer's trumpet great excitement was seen throughout the town. As one illustration of the value of the Pilchard fishery in those early days, in 1838, 13,558 hogsheads were exported from St. Ives to Italy. I also remember a great stir in the town because some men insisted upon fishing on Sundays.

Another very interesting matter was a Parliamentary Election, particularly if there was a contest, and if so there arose a great deal of angry feeling.

Bands of music on both sides continually paraded the streets, accompanied by flags and banners. On orders from the candidates, every man, woman, and child was presented with flags and rosettes, but my memory does not tell me that these were ever paid for, at any rate by the defeated candidate.

In those days there was no Ballot Act, so after the election the voting list was very minutely examined by both sides ; and any voter's name found on the wrong side from the examiner's point of view, had at once a black mark placed against it, and if by chance he happened to be a tradesman, a very strong hint was given him as to future dealings with him.

At one election a rather interesting case arose, there being two candidates, a Mr. Vivian, " Liberal," and a Mr. Paul, " Conservative."

Just at that time there came to St. Ives a new Comptroller of Customs, whose politics none knew. This gentleman went to Mr. Paul's agent (Mr. Robert Bamfield, solicitor) and said, " You are aware just now that there is a question if Government officials are entitled to vote ; do you think I should be safe in voting for Mr. Paul ? " The agent promptly replied, " Most certainly ; I will take all responsibility." Then as a rejoinder the wily officer said, " If I can vote for Mr. Paul, I can vote for Mr. Vivian, and I will do so."

1845. Another point of interest I call to mind. In 1845 Ireland suffered severely from a potato famine, which caused serious mortality from sheer starvation ; consequently, a day of humiliation was ordered, and special services were held at all places of worship. I well remember attending one of them.

Here I might say something of the early history

of railways. Two of the first in the kingdom were in Cornwall, one known as the old West Cornwall, and the other the Bodmin and Wadebridge.

The former ran from Hayle to Redruth, and the Hayle Station was under the present main line (Hayle Viaduct). At that time it was considered dangerous for the locomotive to come up to the station, so the train was drawn by horses from the Phillack side (the old line can still be seen). The trains proceeded over Angarrack Hill, at the top of which was a stationary engine; a rope was used to pull up and let down the trains over the incline. I have an impression there were no covers to the coaches, and only movable seats, and I well remember as a lad being taken to Camborne by train, when on the return journey the rope parted, and some passengers were injured.

1848. In 1848 I was confirmed at Lelant Parish Church, by the then Bishop of Exeter (Bishop Henry Phillpotts).

As to the Bodmin and Wadebridge Line, at that time I knew little of it, but I heard an amusing story about it. One day a lady passenger complained to the guard of the excessive shaking of the carriages, which he admitted. Shortly after there was an improvement, on which she congratulated him. His answer was, " Yes, we are off the line now."

I have heard in my time many amusing tales of Cornish railway passengers, not only in the old days but also in the present day.

When the Chacewater and Newquay Line was opened, there were many people in that district who had never travelled by train. On one occasion a woman asked for a ticket for Mary Tavy, a station on the South Devon Line ; the next woman, under the impression that that was the correct mode, asked for a ticket for Jane Peters ; another woman asked for a single to Plymouth, and the next said, married to Liskeard.

At the opening of the South Western Line to Delabole, a woman came to the stationmaster and requested him to keep a seat for her in the one o'clock train the next day. Her request was complied with.

When she came to the station on the following day, she found the train had left five minutes. Speaking sharply to the stationmaster she said, "Well, if you are going to be so particular as that, all I can tell you is, you won't do much trade down here."

Again, speaking of Cornish people in the old days, I am reminded of a Cornish gentleman appointed a magistrate, who like a wise man went to Bodmin to see how justice was administered there. It happened to be Assize Day, when a man tried for murder was found guilty, and sentenced to be hanged, with the usual formula.

The first case that came before the new magistrate was that of a man charged with being drunk and disorderly. In addressing the prisoner, he said, " You are to be taken to the place from whence you came, etc., etc." The clerk remarked to the magistrate, " You cannot do that, sir ; the penalty is only 40s." The magistrate, in his most judicial voice, said, " Prisoner, we have reconsidered your sentence ; you are fined 40s. and costs, and may the Lord have mercy on your soul."

1855. Again referring to my going to London, in July, 1855, on my arrival there, I at once obtained a situation in a large city warehouse, at the munificent salary of £25 per annum.

In the month of the following November I was summoned to the counting-house, and told that the principal partner had given orders that the staff was to be reduced during the winter; accordingly I was presented with a month's salary, and with several others walked out.

Previous to leaving, one of the junior partners came to me and said he had no voice in it; I pointed out to him that a great injustice had been done, after working early and late through the busy season, to be turned out on a miserable London November foggy morning to seek a situation.

He outwardly expressed much sympathy, and gave me a letter of introduction to a Bristol firm (which letter I still have), but I came to the decision to cease all connection with the drapery for ever.

I had no alternative but to return to St. Ives, where fortunately, accompanied by my father, I was favoured with an interview with Mr. Henry Lewis Stephens, then residing at Tregenna Castle, and, through him, I obtained a situation with the London and South Western Railway Company.

Returning for one moment to living in a large city warehouse, it was certainly a peculiar experience to a lad from a small country town, mixing with a great number of young fellows of all sorts from every part of the kingdom.

At first, although amused, I was also interested in their several discussions, finding there were only a few who were not prepared to advise the Government on any difficult question.

The principal subject discussed at that time was the fighting of General Garibaldi for Italian Unity, which ended in the creation of the Kingdom of Italy.

I saw the General driving through London after his great success.

It would take too much space to record the sayings and doings of hundreds of young men engaged in a large warehouse.

There is, however, one case I remember of a country lad coming to our warehouse seeking a situation. He saw one of our buyers, and in a Cornish way, asked if he might see the top of the house. Knowing quite well the lad meant one of the partners, the buyer said, " Certainly " ; and, after taking the lad up several flights of stairs, with a smile, remarked, " This is the top of the house."

About this time it was the rage for young men to have their hair cut very short.

One young man, a friend of mine, went down to Bristol for a week-end, and on the Sunday at church he was surprised to find every one hesitated to sit in the same pew. After the service, numerous questions were asked by his relatives as to how long the fever had left him, and some, less charitable, were a little suspicious as to his late residence.

One of the buyers in the same warehouse went through a similar tonsorial process. On seeing him the manager asked, " Are you busy upstairs, Mr. C. ? " " Not very, sir." " Then go and get your likeness taken, nail it on this pillar, write on it ' to be seen alive upstairs '—that will fetch them up if anything will."

1856. With other numerous London attractions, young men from the city warehouses were fond of going to the then noted Evans' in Covent Garden, where they could get a very inexpensive supper. It was indeed a pleasant change from the daily warehouse routine, and as there was some good glee singing by young choristers from several churches, the supper-room was a very desirable rendezvous, and was the original of Thackeray's Cave of Harmony in "The Newcomes."

But there was one point to be careful about, that was, to be ready with your statement of what you had partaken, as there was a very general impression that whilst you were hesitating, the cashier was adding a penny ; but it generally finished with, "fifteen pence is one and five."

In speaking of dining-rooms, there are two cases I should like to mention.

During the many years I was engaged in the City, I continually visited one very well-known dining-room. After a time, for some reason the proprietor advanced the prices. I complained to the head waiter, that I thought regular customers should be treated better. His answer was, "It is not for such as you, sir ; it is on account of the country people, who come here so empty that you can hear it drop."

Occasionally I went to what was well known as a "fish ordinary" at Billingsgate, the fish certainly was of the best, but what amused me was that when all was ready, and everybody seated, the proprietor would enter and march to the top of the table, and in one breath, say, "For what we are about to receive may the Lord make us truly thankful there is boiled salmon fried soles and fried eels."

CHAPTER II

1856. I WAS sent for by the South Western Railway Company, and entered Waterloo Station on the first of January, 1856. I went on trial in the Booking Office for one month, at the expiration of which I was duly appointed on the staff as a booking clerk.

I might here mention that having very early as well as late duty, it was very necessary to reside near the station. I did so ; my landlord was connected with the penny boats, well known at that time, that ran between London and Westminster Bridges. The boats ran continuously from daylight to dark, Sundays as well as week days, consequently the children of the crew, being asleep when work ceased, scarcely ever saw their fathers. He said he had often seen mothers bring their children to the pier, and on the arrival of a boat, say to a child, " There, that is your father, the one with a straw hat."

It is quite impossible for me to give anything like an adequate description of the enormous changes in railway travelling from that time to the present.

In the old days there were no lunch or lavatory coaches, but there were so-called express trains, for which extra fares were charged ; some went forty miles an hour, a speed considered rather excessive.

There were no Westinghouse brakes, no communication between driver and passengers in case of need ; generally, the only signal was on the station platform, with a distant signal, at some distance at each side, and one could see sparks flying caused by the brakes.

Now, the driver is able to run into the various stations at thirty to forty miles an hour, and with comparative safety, in spite of the largely increased number of trains at the present day.

As to the carriages, those then in use appear to have been copies from the old road coaches, and a carriage of a present express train would make four of them.

Passengers' luggage was carried on the roof, the guards on many trains rode outside in a kind of sentry-box, called by them a " booby hutch."

On some Great Western trains a man rode in a covered box on the engine tender, with his back to the driver, thus having a good view of the train in case of need on its journey.

In those early days, third class passengers were not treated with the attention and comfort that they receive at the present time.

The 3rd class or Parliamentary train at 1d. per mile was generally timed to start from London stations at a most inconvenient hour.

Speaking of my own experience, I have frequently gone to Waterloo Station about 6 a.m. and found the booking office crowded with third class passengers on bitter cold winter mornings.

As before stated, there being no Cornwall railway, Cornish passengers as a rule had to travel via Bristol, but the third class train from Paddington did not arrive at Bristol in time to catch the steamer for Cornwall ; however, there was a fairly fast train just before from Paddington that took third class passengers for stations on the Bristol and Exeter Line, so Cornish passengers took third class tickets for one of their stations and alighted at Bristol.

This being discovered, no third class was issued above Bridgwater, thus making a third to Bridgwater equal to a second to Bristol.

I do not say that the duties of a booking clerk in those days were particularly onerous ; there were fewer trains, but the work was very exacting, not only because of the very large amounts taken in a short time, but also on account of the care required not to book a passenger for a non-stopping station, and, moreover, the clerk was held responsible for all errors.

As the season advanced Sunday became the heaviest day, excursion trains being run to Southampton, Portsmouth, Salisbury, and the Isle of Wight, etc., to which places passengers were conveyed in carriages without windows.

On Sunday mornings, after the departure of the excursion trains, some time was spent in counting the cash, then home for breakfast and the needful wash-up.

There was no time for church ; and, as at that time trains did not leave the terminus on Sundays during church hours, the spare time was taken up in visiting the tobacco shops for small change, so as to meet the Sunday afternoon pleasure seekers for Kew Gardens, Hampton Court, Windsor, and other favourite resorts.

1856. Shortly after being at Waterloo Station, the Railway Companies decided to register passengers' luggage to the Continent, and as I had, "or was supposed to have had," a smattering of French, I was appointed for that duty.

A few weeks later another change took place. The Staines and Wokingham Line was just completed, and although a separate company, it was to be worked by the South Western Company. The line ran from Staines to Wokingham, thence over the South Eastern Line, and into their Reading Station.

Again I received instructions to proceed to Reading to take charge of the South Western interests, and on my arrival there I was reminded that under the Act of Parliament I had no outdoor powers at the station. From that time I could clearly see there was trouble ahead, and it came.

As mentioned before, the Great Western Company did not encourage third class passengers, and ran only one third class train.

The second return fare, Reading and Paddington, was 6s. 8d., but the South Eastern Railway Company ran a fairly fast train to London Bridge Station at 4s. 6d. return, although the distance was sixty-six miles, against thirty-six to Paddington. There being no Underground at that time from Paddington to the City, passengers reached the City at less cost and nearly as quickly as via Paddington.

1857. Watching this state of things for some time, I decided to put the matter before the General Manager at Waterloo Station. I did so, and as a result received instructions to issue similar 4s. 6d. tickets by our first train ; consequently, our distance to Waterloo Station being only forty-four miles, the journey was covered in less time, and we soon had the bulk of the passengers.

Seeing how matters stood, the South Eastern Company made a further reduction which I followed, till eventually both companies came down to 1s. 3d. single and 2s. return. These fares continued for, I think, some two years. On

Sundays we generally had two or three crowded trains.

The result of all this competition caused me extreme inconvenience ; I was forbidden to use the office after the departure of our trains.

As I failed to foresee any improvement in my position, I asked for a change, which was refused ; I then sent in my resignation, and this was also refused.

Eventually the three companies met and decided to revise the fares and to pool the earnings, an arrangement which, I think, is still in force.

1858. There is one important point I must mention. In those days Reading held a very large pleasure and horse fair, and at one of them I had secured a number of horses for conveyance to London, for whose accommodation I had down a good supply of horse-boxes.

Returning one day from the fair, I, found the South Eastern Stationmaster had taken some of the boxes, and being naturally annoyed, I have no doubt I made use of very strong language.

After the departure of their train, a gentleman (a perfect stranger) came to me and asked me what was the trouble just now between the Station master and myself. I replied, " Really, sir, I do not think it has anything to do with you." His answer was, " Perhaps not ; only I am the Chairman of the South Western Railway Company." Of course I at once explained all the case, and I have no hesitation in saying that Mr. Chaplin (of the firm of Chaplin and Horne) never forgot me.

I should have mentioned before that at the time I joined the South Western Company, in 1856, the Crimean War was just over. I well remember the great excitement there was at Waterloo Station when Peace was declared.

c

To celebrate it, there was a great Naval Review at Spithead, when a number of special trains were provided, not only for the Crown Ministers and Members of both Houses of Parliament, but also for the general public.

The demand for seats was enormous, and very considerable difficulty was caused in keeping separate trains for each party. I was engaged in the issue of tickets, special police being appointed for the examination of the invitation cards.

In one case the War Minister (Lord Panmure) came without an invitation card and the police refused to allow him to pass, upon which he said who he was. The policeman at once remarked, " Oh, no, that won't do, we have had him here several times to-day."

I well remember the magnificent illuminations throughout London, and the excitement of the enormous crowds in the streets on the return of the Guards from the Crimea.

About this time I had my first experience of telegraphy, and on being admitted into the telegraph office and shown the instrument at work, the clerk asked if I would like to ask a question at any station ; I did so of Portsmouth, and was astonished at receiving an answer in one minute.

Hailing from a small country town, a cry of fire was something startling to me. One Sunday evening I was told there was a fire to be seen near, so I left the office to see it.

At that moment a London policeman came up, whose first words were, " What, a fire now, and not near quarter day ! "

In speaking of fires, I may here mention that I saw Covent Garden Theatre burnt to the ground.

1858. When residing at Reading, there was a

deal of correspondence in the papers about tips to railway servants; accordingly, the General Manager of the South Eastern Railway Company issued a circular to his staff to the effect that any servant of the Company seen to demand or receive a tip from a passenger was to be instantly dismissed.

One evening I was on the platform just before the departure of a train, when I saw a guard receive sixpence from a lady in a carriage. On turning round the guard at once saw that the stationmaster had also seen it, so he forthwith rushed to the bookstall, bought a newspaper and took it to the lady together with the change. I said to the guard, Barrett by name, " That was a narrow shave for you." His answer was, " Well, sir, I do not care what trouble I get into so long as I get out."

I do not think for one moment that railway officers are more intelligent than other people, and I have a recollection of one case to the contrary.

A stationmaster was promoted District Super-intendent ; one of his first acts was to recommend at Headquarters that a weigh-bridge should be provided at one of his stations. He was requested to send particulars as to position, size, etc. After forwarding the necessary details, he was told that the size he suggested was not large enough to take such articles as furniture vans, and similar vehicles. He replied that the difficulty could be overcome by weighing the front wheels first, and the hind wheels after.

1859. When residing at Reading I frequently visited a dining-room kept by a Mr. Martin, at 1 p.m. for lunch. The " Times " newspaper was then a speciality, and there was an old gentleman who got there about 12.45 daily to secure the paper. No other person had any chance of seeing it, and although many hints were thrown out matters did not improve. At length one waggish customer had a card printed, "Gentlemen who come here to learn to spell should take yesterday's papers." This had the desired effect.

This Mr. Martin was a very interesting character, and would insist on joining in any conversation taking place between his customers.

At this time the noted *Great Eastern* steamer was ready for launching, a task of considerable difficulty, and discussions were rife on the subject. Mr. Martin expressed his views by stating that he did not think she would float long, for at Margate last week he saw waves rolling in quite as high as his room.

Remarking that probably it was a spring tide, his answer was, "My dear sir, what is the use of your speaking of spring tides, as this was in October."

I would here mention that in those days, 1858, the *Great Eastern* steamship was considered a marvel in shipbuilding, being 680 feet long, and 18,918 tons.

As I have mentioned the *Great Eastern* steamship, I might say that at this time there was considerable interest taken in the subject of telegraphic communication between Europe and America. In 1857, a Mr. Cyrus Field, a prominent American merchant, came to England to explain his scheme, which, however, was very coldly received.

In 1857, the first attempt was made, and I am under the impression the *Great Eastern* was one of the vessels engaged in 1865 ; but the vessels only got three hundred miles from land when the cable broke.

In the following summer another cable was laid, and was at work two or three days, during which congratulatory messages passed between Queen Victoria and the President of the United States ; it then failed through faulty insulation.

In 1865, a further attempt proved unsuccessful.

However, in 1866 the feat was accomplished, and I recollect very well that considerable satisfaction was manifested not only in London but also in the country at such a splendid result.

The submarine cable, which was certainly of marvellous construction, was manufactured by Messrs. Siemens Brothers. They presented me with a sample portion, showing its construction from its smallest details to its final completion. This I still have in my possession.

At the time I refer to, the South Western Railway was very small compared to what it is to-day ; the extent of it was Portsmouth, Southampton, Weymouth, and Salisbury, with Windsor, Reading, and two or three minor branches.

Some years ago the late Mr. Chaplin gave me a copy of one of the first directors' reports, prepared before the line was opened.

In it there were calculations as to the future earnings, from a record kept of the number of passengers carried by the old stage coaches. This interesting report I regret to say I have lost.

The Reading of to-day is very different from the time I was there ; the well-known and eminent firm of Huntley and Palmer was much smaller ; I think I am correct in saying at that time they had a small retail shop in London Street, which business was afterwards removed to the Market Place.

At the present time Reading has a population of 90,000.

I am reminded of a rather amusing incident which occurred at a Liberal political meeting, attended by me, in the London Street Hall.

The sitting Member was Sir Henry Keating, Q.C., afterwards a Judge of the High Court, and a young Barrister came down to oppose him.

At the meeting the opposition was most vigorously taken up by the Right Hon. Sir Robert Phillimore, father of the present Sir Walter, late Lord Justice of Appeal.

At the meeting a gentleman arose and proposed that Mr. Bourne should take the chair, remarking that he was sure that Mr. Bourne would have great pleasure in doing so.

Thereupon Mr. Bourne sprang up and said, " The gentleman who proposed I should take the chair, said he was quite sure I would do so with great pleasure, but there are many degrees of pleasure."

" A few days ago my wife presented me with a boy ; accordingly, I went to the Reading ' Mercury ' Office and gave particulars for an insertion. On leaving I was re-called and asked for 7s. 6d. ; I said I thought no charge was made ; the clerk replied, ' We charge for births, but we will insert your death with pleasure.' "

At the time I was stationed at Reading executions were conducted in public. My office was directly opposite the gaol, but as my tastes did not run in the direction of public hanging, I did not see any, although by chance I once saw the gallows erected for one.

At this time there was no narrow gauge on the Great Western Line to Paddington, so all their traffic from stations north of Wolverhampton for

London had to be changed from narrow to broad gauge trucks at that station.

To meet this difficulty, a short junction was made near the station under the Great Western main line, thus enabling narrow-gauge trucks from their northern stations to get to London over the South Western Line to Nine Elms Station.

In connection with this new service I was instructed to visit the principal stations in the north of England.

Returning for one moment to my early residence in London, it is almost impossible for one to think of London as it was then, and as it is to-day, and of the enormous increase in its size and population north, south, east, and west.

At that time there was scarcely a house between Wandsworth and Vauxhall stations, whereas to-day Wandsworth has a population of some 380,000 and Battersea 170,000.

The Surrey, Vauxhall, and Cremorne Gardens, all noted places of resort, were virtually considered in the country, and I was favoured with a free ticket between Waterloo and Vauxhall stations to enable me to have a country walk when off duty. Earl's Court and West Kensington were market gardens.

The same may be said of East London; for instance, East Ham, when the Royal Albert Dock was commenced, had its parish church in the fields and almost alone, and to-day East Ham has a population of 160,000.

One day the vicar of the parish called on the Dock Contractor and asked him if he could get some of the hundreds of workmen whom he employed to come to church on Sunday.

On the following Sunday, much to the surprise of the vicar, the church was quite full. The grateful vicar proceeded to thank his friend the contractor, and asked him how he did it. His reply was, " I gave them a pint of beer each."

1859. Whilst retaining Reading as my headquarters, I was frequently called on to fill temporary positions.

In 1859 the South Western opened their line from Salisbury to Exeter; it was a single line throughout, and the opening was generally considered a little premature.

One Sunday I was summoned to Waterloo Station. On arriving there the General Manager instructed me to proceed to Exeter, as there was some indication of trouble at the Honiton Tunnel. I went to Exeter the same night, and on the following day information reached me that as a result of a very severe thaw, the earth on the top of the tunnel was slipping and all traffic blocked. I at once proceeded there, and found such was the case, but it was much worse some little distance on the London side. Not only the railway bank, but also some farm buildings as a whole slid down, the line being blocked for some time, and consequently a large number of coaches and other vehicles had to be obtained for the transfer of passengers and their luggage to and from a temporary siding and the next passenger station. This continued for several weeks.

I will mention another incident when at Reading. I had never before been in a Court of Justice, so one day as the Assizes were on I went.

The case tried was a dispute as to the proceeds from the sale of a race-horse; Baron Wilde was the Judge, Piggot, Q.C., was for plaintiff, and Huddleston, Q.C., for defendant.

The former opened his case in what seemed to me a most convincing speech, and in my innocence of law, I thought it absurd to continue the case. However, when plaintiff went into the box, the first question put to him by Huddleston was, "What is your name?" He gave an answer. Huddleston said, "No, no, what was your name when you were convicted at Shrewsbury?" I at once left the Court with a fixed determination to hear both sides in future before coming to a decision.

On another occasion I was instructed to go down and make a general survey for traffic purposes of the Somerset and Dorset Railway District, then a separate company, but afterwards purchased by the South Western and Midland Companies.

I was accompanied by another South Western officer, who proved most amusing and interesting as a companion. He died many years ago.

We never finished breakfast without his asking where we should be about one o'clock for lunch. In passing through Glastonbury, he noticed an obelisk in the market square, and on seeking information as to the reason of its erection from a tradesman standing at his shop door, the man replied, "I don't know, sir, but I think it was to fill up a gap."

Speaking of Glastonbury, I once saw Blondin performing on the tight rope in the Abbey Grounds.

1861. I was appointed the City Superintendent for the South Western Railway Company in 1861, a position I held for seventeen years.

It is not my intention, nor is it possible for me to recollect or record, the innumerable matters of general public interest which took place during that lengthy period.

I will only mention a few with which I was

more or less connected, or in which I was interested, although many are still fresh in my memory.

In 1861, the year in which Prince Albert died, I remember passing through the Strand that night, and hearing the great bell of St. Paul's tolling.

In a previous note I mentioned the time when General Garibaldi was fighting for Italian Unity. Happily his work was crowned with success, and in April, 1861, the Conqueror came to London, where his reception was marvellous ; on his arrival in the metropolis some thirty thousand working men formed a procession ; I saw the General in it, in his usual scarlet coat.

About this time there were wars in various parts of the world, but the most serious, as far as England was concerned, was the outbreak of the American Civil War in 1861, arising partly from the jealousy of the North on account of the great success of the Southern trade, as well as from the great desire of the Northern States of America for the abolition of slavery, and from the feelings of the people being deeply stirred by the publication of Mrs. Ward Beecher Stowe's " Uncle Tom's Cabin "—a book of an enormous circulation, said to be exceeded only by the Bible.

However, in 1864, as a result of the war, a Bill was passed whereby slavery in the United States was abolished for ever.

Arising out of that war were many things which caused very considerable stir not only in London, but also throughout the country, especially the seizure of the Confederate Commissioners on the British Steamer *Trent*, the escape of the Confederate steamer *Alabama* from Birkenhead, and the terrible sufferings in Lancashire caused by the cotton famine, for the alleviation of which a general subscription was set on foot in 1862, which reached the sum of £2,235,000.

1862. In the same year the second great Exhibition was held in London, which I had to attend in my official capacity.

In connection with the present Great War, there is one point of interest worthy of note with respect to that Exhibition.

The French had considerable space allotted them, and obtained permission to enclose it.

The Prussians complained, but the French held their ground, saying that they would not have themselves put out of the way for a semi-barbarous people beyond the Rhine.

1863. In 1863 Princess Alexandra arrived from Denmark for her marriage to the Prince of Wales. I cannot forget the great reception she received on her passage over London Bridge and through the City.

On the 10th March the wedding took place at Windsor, but I am afraid that few of the present generation will remember the affection shown on that occasion to the late King Edward and the Princess.

There are numerous amusing and interesting anecdotes one could mention, if space permitted, in connection with railway officers and railway working.

I well remember the late Sir Richard Moon telling me, when Chairman of the London and North Western Railway Company, of a peculiar case. On one occasion in constructing a new line they had to make a very high embankment, when an action was brought against them by an adjoining mill-owner for obstructing the wind required for his mill. Strange to say before the trial came on the mill was blown down.

Also in railway Parliamentary matters much might be said.

Sir Richard also told me of a case where the Great Western Company had given notice for promoting a line to one of their stations (I think it was Aylesbury); his Board were up in arms about it, and were prepared to spend any amount to defeat the Great Western.

On his pointing out the present earnings at that station, and the probable cost of the opposition, which would exceed more than ten years' present earnings, they gave way, and they were then getting from the Great Western five times the traffic they had before.

One General Manager once told me, "of course in strict confidence," that if he were going to Parliament to poach on another company's preserves, he would try to get a Radical chairman and committee of the House of Commons, but if he had to stop another company poaching on his district, he would try to get a House of Lords Conservative chairman and committee.

In the early history of railways there was considerable discussion as to the relative advantages of the narrow gauge and the broad, known as the Battle of the Gauges.

Many years ago I was travelling with a very stout gentleman, who had been engaged in railway surveying. He described to me the great difficulties and opposition he had frequently experienced, having often to work by night, and with the aid of lamps. He said, in one case on going over a lady's estate, she sent her servant to tell him of her objection, and she asked him was he broad gauge or narrow. He said, " Madam, personally I am broad, but I am surveying for the narrow." She laughed and said, " Then go on."

When residing in London, as a Cornishman I felt it my duty to join the Cornish Dinner Committee, whose annual banquet was a very interesting event, and gave one an opportunity of meeting many Cornish people living in London.

Unfortunately at first ladies were not admitted to the annual dinners, so after a time I moved a resolution to admit them.

In spite of considerable opposition, the resolution was eventually carried, and those most antagonistic to the presence of the fair sex soon afterwards admitted their error.

The Annual Dinner of Cornishmen in London may rightly be regarded as the parent of the London Cornish Association of which I was elected the first chairman, and I know that at present as in the past it continues to do good work for young men from Cornwall.

During the winter months there were frequent musical entertainments, conversaziones, and exceedingly interesting lectures were given. I must refer to one important lecture, given by the Rev. S. Baring-Gould on " Cornwall a Thousand Years Ago."

At the close of the lecture the late Mr. Passmore Edwards proposed a vote of thanks to the lecturer, which was jocosely seconded by the Rev. Joseph Hocking. In the course of his remarks he said, " I have heard what the rev. gentleman has told us of the serfdom of the Cornish women in the old days, and of their emancipation in modern days, but the fact remains that both the rev. gentleman and myself were so afraid of them that we went to Yorkshire for our wives."

Mr. Hocking also added : There was a Cornish wife who went to a market town, and during her absence her husband ventured to invite some of his friends to his house. In a discussion which followed, he said, " Are you masters in your own house ? I am ; they know it as soon as I put my foot on the doorstep ; I am Julius Cæsar here." At that moment the door opened and his wife entered and said, " Why are you not in bed ? Go at once."

At a musical entertainment of which I was chairman, one of the vocalists came late and apologised for his unpunctuality by treating us to the following tale.

On his way to the hall he said he met a gentleman whom he had not seen for some years.

In the course of conversation the singer asked him if he were married, and the answer being in the affirmative, remarked that it was good. " Not so good, she brought me no money," said he. " That was bad," replied the vocalist. " Not so bad, for she brought a flock of sheep." " That was good." " Not so good, for a large number were diseased." " That was bad." " Not so bad, as we boiled them down for their tallow." " That was good." " Not so good, for the tallow overflowed and burned down the building." " That was bad." " Not so bad, as my wife's mother went with it."

CHAPTER III

IN 1866 a new ministry came into power with Lord John Russell as Prime Minister. He at once brought in a Bill for the extension of the franchise, which met with defeat, and in consequence a serious riot took place in London; the mob proceeded to Hyde Park, and tore down the railings. Out of curiosity I visited the Park and saw the damage done by the rioters.

1867. In 1867 there were many serious Fenian outrages in various parts of England and Ireland. One perhaps more violent than the rest was an attempt to blow up Clerkenwell Prison, where two men were confined under remand. A rebel placed a barrel of gunpowder against the wall, and set it alight.

I was standing at my office door at the time, but my pen fails me in attempting to give anything like an adequate description of the feeling of resentment caused by such rioters. Rumours soon got about, and it was freely circulated that the Bank of England and the Tower of London were destroyed.

Anyhow, it is pleasant to record that the glaring outrage on Clerkenwell Prison failed to set the prisoners free.

In 1868 numerous other Fenian outrages took place, one especially being an attempt on the " Times " Office.

I think there is no doubt that these outrages

in a great measure led Mr. Gladstone to take seriously into consideration the Irish Church Disestablishment, but this is a subject I refrain from discussing except to state that at that period I was favoured with a free use of the Lobby of the House of Commons, and many very stirring debates I have listened to, and witnessed many uproarious scenes on the Irish question.

In 1870 the Franco-German War broke out; I remember well that day. In the evening I was attending to my duties at the Royal Exchange, when the news was posted that France had declared war on Germany.

It was certainly unexpected, for I have a distinct recollection that, at a public dinner a day or two before, one of the prominent Government officials stated that the political horizon was particularly clear.

I am not going into the causes or progress of that war, for history has fully dealt with it.

1871. There is, however, one matter of a personal nature I will refer to. On the fall of Paris there was a general desire in England to send help in the way of provisions to the starving people of that city, and I arranged with Messrs. Rothschild to take over for them a cargo of flour from Southampton to Havre; but, on arrival there, it was found that the French had sunk some ships in the river Seine, to prevent the Germans from getting to Paris by water, so the flour was landed at Havre to await events.

At the time I was at Havre the Germans were just outside, and the deplorable condition of the place, as I saw it, will never be effaced from my memory.

In addition to my varied and numerous duties

as City Superintendent for the South Western Railway Company, I took considerable interest in the development of shipping traffic at Southampton Docks ; at that time it was a private company, and very different from the present Docks. The South Western Company acquired the Docks some time ago.

However, after innumerable visits to Liverpool, Glasgow, Cork, Bristol, and other ports, I eventually succeeded in getting some of the largest shipping companies to avail themselves of the advantages of Southampton as a port, a venture which proved a success.

I am not sure, but I think I was, if not the first, at any rate one of the first to get live cattle and chilled meat imported to this country from America.

1869. The opening of the Suez Canal in 1869 caused a revolution in respect not only to docks but also more particularly to the large shipping firms trading with the Far East.

Previous to the opening of the Suez Canal, the P. and O. Company ran small steamers between Alexandria and Southampton, carrying very valuable goods, which had been conveyed across from Suez to Alexandria.

At that time cargoes were satisfactorily dealt with at Southampton ; but, on the opening of the Canal, all was changed.

If my memory serves me rightly the first P. & O. steamer from the East was the *Australia*, with a cargo of tea. Here a difficulty at once arose, for tea, being under bond, not only required railway trucks under the Customs' locks, but also the conveyances between the London station and the City bonded warehouses.

To meet this I at once secured a large number

D

of furniture vans, having the necessary locks, and thus satisfied the Custom authorities.

The steadily increasing size of steamers began to affect all docks, particularly Southampton, for which port goods were as a rule on through Bills of Lading, and then came the question for the shipowners' consideration which was the better, to discharge at Southampton and pay the railway carriage to London, or to steam there direct. Of course, the larger the cargo the worse for the docks ; I admit that since the docks have come into the possession of the South Western Company large cargoes have been discharged at Southampton Docks ; but the steamers also bringing a large number of passengers and then passing over the railway enabled the company to offer the shipowner very considerable advantages.

1869. The Holborn Viaduct was opened by H.M. Queen Victoria in 1869, a notable event of which I have a very vivid recollection. Few people of the present generation can have the faintest idea of the advantages arising from the erection of the present magnificent structure, and of the gain to that district, more especially with regard to its vehicular traffic. It superseded the deep dip of the two hills into the valley of the Fleet river.

1871. In the latter part of 1871 great gloom was cast not only over London, but also throughout the Empire, in consequence of the very serious illness of the Prince of Wales, afterwards King Edward VII.

Every edition of the papers was at once bought and eagerly read, but on the 8th December a grave relapse took place, and for several days special prayers were offered in every place of worship for his recovery. Fortunately a turn for the better took place, and the recovery of the Prince was so marked, that on the 27th February the Queen and Prince Consort, accompanied by other members of the Royal Family, attended a service of Thanksgiving at St. Paul's. I had the pleasure of having a seat in Ludgate Hill. In the evening St. Paul's and the principal streets were magnificently illuminated.

1872. The Ballot Act, to which I have alluded before, was passed in 1872, whereby open voting for Members of Parliament ceased.

1873. London was favoured in 1873 by a visit from the Shah of Persia. I was fortunately present at his arrival on the 18th June, and he certainly became of considerable interest to Londoners.

1878. In the latter part of 1878 the London and St. Katharine Docks Company advertised for an assistant General Manager. I made application for the position, and from a large number of candidates was appointed, thus bringing my twenty-three years' service with the South Western Railway Company to a close. On tendering my resignation the General Manager sent for me and expressed his regret at my leaving after so many years of close connection.

In course of conversation he said there was an old saying, " You had better put up with the ills ye know, than fly to those ye know not of." However, we parted good friends, and remained so to his death.

Before I finish as to my connection with the South Western Railway Company, there is one subject I should like to refer to. While engaged in the City I occasionally attended the Easter Vestry meeting and I was astonished to see what little interest was taken by the public. Although the meetings were held in connection with one of the principal City churches, there were seldom more than two or three parishioners present. I once asked the clerk, was it always thus; his answer was, " Yes, since we discontinued putting on the notice, Lunch at 1 p.m."

1879. I joined the Docks Company in February, 1879. At that time there were in London four principal dock companies, viz. the London and St. Katharine, the East and West India, the Millwall on the north of the Thames, and the Surrey Commercial on the south side, amongst which there was very keen competition, and it had been evident for some time that, with the fast-increasing size of steamers, the present docks were becoming obsolete ; consequently, the London and St. Katharine Company promoted and obtained an Act for the building of a new dock, now known as the Royal Albert Dock.

Before referring at present to the new dock, I will deal with those at the time I joined.

(1) The St. Katharine Docks occupy a space of twenty-three acres and store very valuable goods from all parts of the world ; their spacious vaults will hold 25,000 pipes of wine and spirits and 4000 tons of oil.

(2) The London Docks adjoining are similarly used, but to a more considerable extent ; their immense vaults, which are a special feature, are capable of holding 50,000 pipes of wine, 60,000 hogsheads of brandy and rum, and thousands of tons of valuable goods.

(3) Cutler St. warehouses occupy four acres, and are largely used for the storing of tea and silk from India, China, and Japan ; the average value of the stock is estimated from £4,000,000 to £5,000,000.

(4) The Royal Victoria Dock is situated just below Blackwall, and some further remarks will be made in its connection with the Royal Albert Dock.

In the Royal Victoria Dock there is warehoused at all times a very large stock of American tobacco, averaging from 25,000 to 30,000 tons, under Customs Bond. With the duty added it is easy to form some idea of its value.

As before mentioned, the opening of the Suez Canal caused considerable change in the ship-building world ; and, as a result, the position and size of entrance of the existing docks were questions that required immediate attention.

At the time I joined, the new dock was getting near its completion, and though I was frequently told that the whole scheme had been most thoroughly worked out, yet its originators had not seen far enough ahead, for even before the dock was opened it was found necessary to make considerable alterations in deepening the entrance and basin.

1880. However, on the 24th June, 1880, the Dock was opened by the Duke and Duchess of Connaught, and named the Royal Albert Dock.

To celebrate its inauguration a large luncheon was provided, and the sitting accommodation for two thousand visitors was so arranged that each faced the Royal table.

To enter fully into the history of the Royal Albert Dock would occupy considerable space ; I do not intend doing so, although a few points may be of interest.

At the time of its opening the Royal Albert, in conjunction with the Royal Victoria, was the largest of the kind in the world ; the length being just three miles, with two entrances from the

Thames, four miles from each other ; and having direct railway communication with all parts of the kingdom.

The Royal Albert Dock has its own passenger line, with four stations, two large dry docks, a hotel and canteens, a postal, money order, and telegraph office ; it is lighted throughout by electric light ; it has two floating cranes capable of lifting fifty and thirty tons respectively ; its tugs are fitted with steam fire-engines ; and the whole of the dock gates, bridges, and cranes are worked by hydraulic machinery, etc., etc.

1888. An Act was passed in 1888 for a working union between the London and East and West India Companies, under the title of the London and India Joint Committee, of which I was appointed Joint Manager, and in 1890 sole Manager.

As the East and West India Dock system, under the 1888 working Act, came under the same management I make some reference to that property, consisting of the West India, East India, and South West India Docks, Crutched Friars and Commercial Road Warehouses, and the recently constructed Tilbury Deep Water Docks. With regard to the latter, it was also evident the East and West India Dock Directors saw clearly that their present system of docks was not at all suitable to meet the ever-increasing size of steamers, so they also obtained an Act for the construction of the Tilbury Docks, which were opened in April, 1886, furnished with all the latest improvements, and, like the Royal Albert, so arranged that passenger and troop trains are enabled to go direct to and from the ship's side.

The warehouses also are utilised for the reception and working of produce of immense value, the organisation and general working being similar to those in vogue at the London and St. Katharine's.

As in the case of the upper docks, owing to the increased size of ships and to their different construction, the entrances to them were more or less obsolete, particularly to the West India Dock, a spacious body of water ; but, as I reported to the Board, like a fine dining-room unable to admit a dining-table, and on my recommendation the Board decided to construct a new entrance with all necessary improvements at a cost of £200,000.

I have before stated that at the time I joined the Docks Company there was very keen competition, not only among the several docks, but also between the private wharfingers and warehouse-keepers.

The latter were in possession of certain advantages over the Dock companies. Lack of space prevents my fully dealing with this matter ; but, it may be stated that at the time the first Dock Act was passed over one hundred years ago, duty was paid on almost everything imported, which therefore did pass over the dock quays, and thus a very large profit accrued to the Dock Company.

But to obtain their Act they waived many valuable points, which now tell against them, as the duty on imported goods has been very much curtailed.

I might here mention that the present Act of the London Port Authority confers wider powers on that Authority than the Dock companies possessed, thus removing many of the difficulties.

However, after considerable negotiations, an agreement was at last arrived at between the several Dock companies and the warehouse-keepers and wharfingers, and for thirteen years

I had the pleasure of presiding as chairman of their meetings.

On my retirement I was presented with a handsome testimonial, bearing the inscription. " Presented to H. W. Williams, Esq., in recognition of his services as Chairman and Member of the Dock, Wharf, Grain, Tea, Wine, and Wool Committee, 11th December, 1900."

There is a point of interest I think I should mention in connection with the present state of Belgium.

At the time I was manager of the Docks, a deputation waited on me, stating that the late King of the Belgians was very desirous that a line of steamers should run daily between Ostend and Tilbury Dock with Belgian produce for the London markets.

On this I paid several visits to Brussels and had numerous interviews with Ministers, and eventually with the assistance of Messrs. Cockerell and Co., the eminent shipbuilders and engineers, a line of steamers was furnished, they left Ostend in time to enable Belgian produce to be delivered in the London markets about 4 a.m. This service continued till the outbreak of the war.

CHAPTER IV

IT is almost an impossibility to give anything like an adequate description of the work to be done in connection with the immense volume of goods continually arriving into the Port, from the discharge at the ship's side until they reach the consumer.

There is in the Docks and warehouses valuable produce from every part of the world ; the general preparation of which, examination for damage and defects, and preparing samples for brokers, etc., entail a very considerable expert knowledge, labour, and expense.

Take one article alone, wool. It has to be conveyed from the ship's side to the warehouse, weighed, and placed in a well-lighted position, in order that each bale may be readily examined by the brokers. During the sales frequently thousands have to be thus treated daily.

1898. Some little idea of the magnitude of the work at the Docks in my last year, 1898, may be gathered from the following :—

	Tons.
Foreign shipping entered the Committee's Docks	4,224,312
Landings of goods for warehousing . . .	1,097,816
Exports passed over the quays	449,596
Stocks of produce on hand at close of the year .	249,898

The above is exclusive of goods in private warehouses.

It must be mentioned that in dealing with such

a vast number of articles of every description the charges are innumerable and very intricate.

The Comptroller of Charges at the Dock House had been in this work for fifty years, and was about to retire. One day he came to my room and asked me my advice as to his future residence. Naturally I suggested the seaside. "Oh no, sir, I cannot do that," said he, "for if I did and saw a ship passing for London, I should at once begin to calculate how much the Dock Company would get out of her. I have had fifty years of that."

In addition to the ordinary work as manager of an enormous undertaking employing many thousands of men, there were at all times important matters requiring one's serious attention, such as Fenian atrocities, Egyptian and South African wars, several dock strikes, and other vital questions.

In dealing with the first it may be asked, "Why should the diabolical work of Fenians in London affect the Docks?" In my answer I pointed out that though the Fenians in 1883 attacked the Local Government Board Office, Scotland Yard, the "Times" Office, and in 1884 continued their dastardly work at several London stations, more particularly at Victoria Station, and later at London Bridge, still they were evidently determined not to allow the Docks to escape their attention.

We received innumerable threats with regard to our Dock entrances, consequently locomotives and tugs were continuously under steam night and day.

On one occasion we received an anonymous letter stating that at a certain hour in the morning an attack would be made on the Volunteer Stand of Arms at the Victoria Dock, that the attention of the Dock Staff would be called off by a fire on the opposite side of the Dock, and that a cart would be in waiting at 3 a.m. to take away the arms.

Realising it was my duty I went down and remained some hours, but nothing unusual took place.

On returning to the office and again reading the letter I was uncertain as to the date, so I went down again that night, and all being quiet till about three o'clock, I decided to return home. Going some distance the police patrol overtook me and stated that the cart was at the Dock entrance ; accordingly I returned and asked the carman why he was there at that early hour, but got no satisfactory answer, only that he was there by order.

Just then a very dense fog came on, and at that moment I could see the reflection of a fire above the fog. I ordered the locomotive and tug to get all ready, but it was impossible to locate the fire. After some time I discovered that the fire was at one of the ship-repairing shops, and had no connection with the threatened fire. We found the owner of the cart, who stated that a stranger had called and paid him a sovereign to take some passenger's luggage to King's Cross Station.

1879. There was the Zulu War.

1881. The Majuba disaster, and defeat of Sir George Colley at Laing's Nek.

1882. The bombardment of Alexandria and defeat of Arabi Pasha at Tel-el-Keber.

1884. General Gordon was shut up at Khartum

1885. An expeditionary force was sent to relieve him : Alas ! too late.

1898. The Arab rebellion in the Soudan.

1899. The outbreak of the great Boer War.

For each of these campaigns special arrangements had to be made not only for troops and horses, but also for officers. I was present at the embarkation of H.R.H. the Duke of Connaught, Lord Wolseley, Lord Methuen, and many others of note.

At the embarkations steamers were not fitted as they are now. Horses had to be lifted on board in horse-boxes.

On one occasion a horse was so restive that it kicked out the bottom of the box and was seriously hurt. I was in some difficulty as to the course to take, when the late Colonel Burnaby standing by said without a moment's hesitation, " Take my charger." I did so and it was placed on board instead of the wounded one.

1899. With reference to the great Boer War, the work necessitated by the embarkation of the enormous number of troops, horses, guns, etc., despatched from London, was exceedingly heavy and trying. I visited the War Office and Admiralty every day, and so successfully did the work proceed that in no case was any one of the great number of transports delayed one hour. At the conclusion I received from the Admiralty the following letter of appreciation :

ADMIRALTY, *27th September*, 1900.

DEAR MR. WILLIAMS,—

In addition to the general letter of thanks sent to the Dock Company by their Lordships, I wish personally to thank you for the very great assistance you have given to this Department in general and to the Divisional Transport Officers at the Docks in particular, at all times during the past year.

I am well aware of all the difficulties you have

had to contend with from time to time, but none had been too great for you to overcome, in the interests of Her Majesty's Services.

I regret to hear of your approaching retirement, and take this opportunity to wish you every happiness in the future.

Believe me,
Yours very truly,
(Signed) BOUVERIE F. CLARK,
Rear Admiral, Director of Transports.

1899. In connection with the Boer War there is a personal matter to which I wish to refer.

At the outbreak of war my younger son, although in a good situation in the City, gave up his post and went to South Africa with the C.I.V.'s under the command of General·Mackinnon. The Regiment left Southampton, 20th January, and arrived at Cape Town 6th February, 1900.

I have a journal he kept in which he says that, on their arrival at Cape Town they went by rail to Orange River Camp, where there was a great gathering of troops awaiting the general advance. His battalion formed part of the 21st Brigade, under General Bruce Hamilton, and at the end of April took part in the memorable march of Lord Roberts to Pretoria, which ended on 5th June, 1900.

His journal treats fully with the difficulties encountered 'en route' particularly with· the lack of food, as well as many other very serious inconveniences.

Feeling that possibly on his return he would not settle down to civil life, at one of my visits to the War Office, I made a request to Lord Lansdowne (then War Minister) to give my son a commission in the regular Army. He said a wire should be sent to Lord Roberts. Three days afterwards I received the following :—

WAR OFFICE,
PALL MALL, S.W.,
October 5th, 1900.

Col. Franklyn presents his compliments to Mr. H. W. Williams and begs to forward him a copy of the telegram received from Lord Roberts with reference to his son, "Sergeant R. M. Williams, City of London Imperial Volunteers " :

(Copy) Sergeant Williams declines Commission in Regular Army.

ROBERTS.

Pretoria,
26th Sept., 1900.

I fail to trace from his journal the exact reason for his refusal of a commission, but it is evident from reading between the lines that at the time it was offered, things were generally unsatisfactory as to rations, clothes, and boots, coupled with many other unpleasantnesses as will be seen from some of the following extracts from his journal.

Whilst continuing my reference to my son's journal, which is particularly interesting reading, I may say I once had the pleasure of submitting it to General Mackinnon on his return to England. He expressed his high appreciation of its contents.

It is quite impossible to give anything but a very meagre account of its contents, but the following extracts are interesting :—

" Sunday, 24th June, very cold nights, blankets frozen hard. I got a pass and went to Church, it was nice to be alone for a bit and the Church was warm, I envied the people as they were leaving for their houses, while I had to wander back on a cold night to the open.

—— I am very hungry, very cold, ice on my blankets.

—— I have not a penny in the world, so I had a walk into the town to try to get some bread but failed.

—— Owing to De Wet having captured our Convoy with our winter clothes we are in a sad plight.

—— Went on guard at General's Head-quarters, got some food from Winston Churchill's cooks, had a good supper.

—— We were paraded for inspection by " Bobs " who said he was very pleased with all we had done.

—— Mackinnon also thanked us personally, it does not go far when hungry.

—— Though I must say, personally, I would not change places with any man, and never regret the step I have taken, it makes you think what a land of plenty England is, and what a little it takes to make you happy when you are on quarter rations.

—— The above extracts are of different dates. I make no reference to any fighting or casualties on that memorable march to Pretoria, as history has recorded all of them.

The journal continues to relate that :—

In the spring of 1902, when in charge of a Block House at Utrecht he received instructions to take Despatches from Lord Kitchener to General Botha. He was accompanied by a Mounted Infantry Patrol and a Guide named Hughes, and was also furnished with a white flag.

After riding the whole day, he met a Boer with a lame horse, who took him to a farm, from which he watched one of our Columns fighting a rearguard action.

He afterwards fell in with an educated Boer named Pluff, a Lieutenant in General Botha's Flying Scouts, to whom he handed his Despatches, and received from him a Boer pass. This pass is in my possession.

Many of the present generation will undoubtedly remember the Black Week of December, 1900, when the British, in their attempts to relieve Ladysmith, Kimberley, and Mafeking received severe repulses at Colenso, Magersfontein, and Stormberg.

Personally, I remember those black days well, for at the frequent sittings of our Board, six of the Directors' sons were at the front, and my son also had been engaged in the war from the commencement.

But on the relief of Ladysmith, Kimberley, and Mafeking, sorrow was turned into joy, and only those living in London at the time can form any idea of the excitement shown.

On the declaration of peace, my son obtained a position in Canada, and early in 1914 was sent from Canada to Singapore.

Shortly after his arrival there, war was declared. He consequently returned to England, and on reporting himself at the War Office, was at once sent to join the Oxford and Bucks Light Infantry as Captain, and has ever since been on active service.

I have in my possession a return of the first 162 transports that left London for South Africa, giving the names of the transports, their tonnage, date of sailing and arrival, as well as full particulars of the troops, horses, guns, etc. conveyed.

In connection with the embarkation of troops for South Africa in the Boer War, there is an interesting case I cannot refrain from mentioning, as it undoubtedly shows the old esprit de corps of the British Army.

I refer to the 1st Royal Dragoons, which embarked in the *Manchester Port* from Tilbury Dock, 31st October, 1899.

The regiment was under the command of Colonel Burn Murdock, now Major-General.

As one of Lord Lansdowne's sons was also an officer going in the same ship, and being informed that his Lordship (then War Minister) intended visiting the steamer before she sailed, I decided to go down with the special troop train, particularly to point out the facilities the dock afforded in the embarkation of troops and horses, in having the train on one side of the shed and the ship on the other, thus passing direct under cover.

The *Manchester Port* was timed to leave the dock at 3 p.m. Just before the appointed hour, I said to the Colonel (perhaps unwisely), " The time is getting short; I see your men are all over the dock ; I want to be quite ready." He looked at me with astonishment and said, " Do you see that lad by my side ? Now when he sounds the Call, if any man is not at once on board, you keep him, he is not worth a —— to me.—Boy, sound the Call." He did so, and the hundreds of men came on board. When they had all arrived, the Colonel said to the officer, " Are they all here ? " He answered, " Yes, every one."

He then turned to me and said, " Now, Mr. Manager, what do you think of that ? " I said I was proud of it. The ship left the dock at 3 p.m.

I have no hesitation in saying that as manager of a great undertaking like the Docks I led a very strenuous life. I recollect on one occasion, when

E

returning from a Board Meeting to my room, saying in a jocular way to my principal assistant, " Is life worth living ? " He said, " Well, sir, if you *have had* lobster salad for supper, I don't think it is ; but, if you *are having* lobster salad for supper, I think it is worth an effort."

Shortly after joining the Dock Company, I received an invitation to join a large party of shipowners and merchants on a trial trip of one of the South African mail steamers, the *Scot*.

The trip finished at Plymouth, and at the final dinner some excellent speeches were made ; with the party was the late Mr. Groser, then very prominently connected with the " Western Morning News," another of the party was the late Mr. Robinson, editor and proprietor of " Fairplay," a very influential City shipping paper.

On the toast list was that of the Press, coupled with the name of Mr. Groser.

I have frequently noticed at public dinners that gentlemen down for speaking pay more attention to their intended speeches than to their dinner ; it was so with Mr. Groser, who sat opposite me, particularly as we were at Plymouth, his own town.

When he rose to respond to the toast, he was most cordially received, and with some excellent remarks eulogized the value of the press, and how it often ruled governments and kingdoms, etc., etc.

On resuming his seat, there was a cry for the editor of " Fairplay," who after a little hesitation rose and in a very humorous way said, " The gentleman who has just spoken told you what to him was the value of the Press, that it ruled governments and kingdoms, but as a pressman, you can take it from me that a great deal you read in some papers is copied from others, and frequently the remainder is concocted in some third floor."

1880. Returning to dock working. Early in 1880 before the use of the refrigerating system came into general use, the Dock Company received an application from an American " gentleman " for permission to utilise a building in the Victoria Dock, to be provided with ice, for the protection of imported chilled meat.

A store was selected, fittings were furnished, and an agreement signed, but when all was complete the American could not be found anywhere.

Some weeks after a serious fire took place, causing, together with many other buildings, the destruction of the ice-store.

To the surprise of all, there forthwith came a claim from the American for damage in consequence of the Dock Company not fulfilling its contract.

1882. I was elected a Fellow of the Royal Geographical Society in 1882, and when residing in London, it gave me great pleasure to attend the lectures during the sessions.

Many of them, that I still have a vivid recollection of, were exceedingly interesting.

(1) At the Royal Albert Hall, in the presence of the late King Edward and Queen Alexandra, then Prince and Princess of Wales, together with several other members of the Royal Family, H. M. Stanley gave us an account of his expedition for the rescue of Emin Pasha.

(2) Captain Fred Selous gave a very interesting account of his explorations in South Africa. I may mention that Selous even at the age of sixty-

three joined the British Forces in East Africa, and at sixty-six, having got the D.S.O., fell fighting for the cause of right.

(3) Fridtjof Nansen, the great Arctic explorer, I heard more than once give an account of his several journeys in the Arctic seas, but I think the most interesting was the description of his push towards the North Pole. He eclipsed all previous records by 3°, and was about a fortnight located on floating ice with no ship on which to fall back ; this still remains in my opinion one of the greatest feats of exploration.

1881–2. Serious troubles continued in Ireland in 1881 and 1882, and eventually culminated in the terrible murders of Lord Frederick Cavendish and Mr. Burke, respectively Secretary and Under Secretary for Ireland, whilst walking in Phœnix Park, Dublin, on Saturday evening the 6th May, 1882. I well remember, when the news was received in London the following Sunday morning, the horror expressed on all sides.

Shortly afterwards I had occasion to visit Dublin, and during my stay, I could not fail to notice the general state of affairs, and the discontent of many of the people. Out of curiosity I visited the spot where Lord Cavendish and Mr. Burke were so foully murdered.

1882. It was also in 1882 that an attempt was made to assassinate Queen Victoria, and there was a certain amount of relief when it became known that the man was insane.

1888. Previously I have stated that there were no free libraries in my early days. In 1888 I was residing at Brentford, and although the Free Libraries Act had been passed, no attempt had been made there to put it into force.

However, a deputation having waited on me

for that purpose, I called a public meeting, where the question was received with great enthusiasm, but a poll was required. This resulted in a victory for the opposition by fifteen votes, and it was astonishing to witness the ignorance of the people with regard to the financial side and limitations of the Act.

The town was circulated by posters warning the public not to be deluded by the penny in the pound story.

But in June, 1889, I presided at another public meeting convened for the same object, and it was decided to put the Act into force, only one voting against it.

The library started in a very modest way, the District Council providing a room; success at once attended it, so much so that in 1902 Mr. Carnegie gave the handsome sum of £5000 for a new building, and to-day this library is one of the best in the kingdom.

·1890. Pressure of work in 1890 compelling me to sever my connection with the library committee, I received the following from the secretary :—

BRENTFORD FREE PUBLIC LIBRARY,
May 5th, 1890.

H. W. WILLIAMS, ESQ.

DEAR SIR,

At a meeting of the General Provisional Committee I was instructed to express regret at your withdrawal, on account of lack of time, from the permanent Committee.

A unanimous vote of thanks was passed for your indefatigable labours as President of that body, for the powerful influence you brought to bear upon the collection of the necessary funds, and the ultimate vote and decision in favour of an

institution, which bids fair to become an inestim-
able blessing to the old County Town of Brentford.

(Signed)   E. PHILLIPS,
Hon. Secretary.

Endorsed by Chairman of General Meeting.
May 2nd, 1890.

Whilst residing in London I frequently paid
a visit to a Turkish bath, and when I did so I
wired my private house as follows : " Going to
bath don't wait for me." On returning home
to my surprise I found the telegram read as
follows, " Going to Death don't wait for me."

I called the Postmaster's attention to it and
received an apology.

In one of my numerous journeys by railway
from Liverpool to London, my fellow-passenger
was a gentleman from New York.

In the course of conversation I said, " Is there
no such thing as casting bread on the waters in
New York ? " He said, " Oh, no, unless the wind
is blowing towards the shore."

CHAPTER V

1887. THE 21st June, 1887, was Queen Victoria's Jubilee day. The Press has faithfully given full particulars of the Royal Procession, of the outburst of loyalty and devotion of the people all along the line of march, and of the splendid display of illuminations.

Fortunately, I was favoured by receiving an invitation card entitling me to a seat in Westminster Abbey, where I witnessed a sight that will never be forgotten ; particularly the entrance into the Abbey of Her Majesty Queen Victoria, the members of the Royal Family, followed by other Royal personages, the most prominent of the latter being the stately Prince Imperial of Germany, husband of our Princess Royal and father of the present Kaiser.

At this moment I distinctly recall the touching scene at the end of the historic service when the members of the Royal Family advanced and did homage to the Queen.

1889. In July, 1889, what was known as the great London Dock Strike took place. It is not my intention, nor do I think it necessary to enter into details as to the cause of the strike or its results, because many of the present generation will recollect it, and the matter has been fully dealt with by the Press.

I intend only to refer to a few of the instances with which I was personally connected, such as the visits from Cardinal Manning, Bishop Temple, and afterwards from some Nonconformist dignitaries. With regard to the latter, I was amused at reading a sermon in the papers by one of them on the previous Sunday (I am afraid I do not remember the exact words), but it was to the effect that he was quite safe as to the future state of the leaders of the strike but not at all certain about the Dock Directors and Manager.

Daily an enormous procession passed the Dock office, the band playing the " Dead March in Saul," headed by Mr. John Burns, Mr. Tom Mann, and Mr. Ben Tillet, accompanied by such trifles as a coffin, effigy, gallows, etc.

In a speech one Sunday on Tower Hill, Mr. John Burns said that Mr. Williams, the manager, was the concentrated quintessence of unadulterated incompetency. Such an unsolicited testimonial, together with numerous threats and anonymous letters I received, did not at any rate add to my spiritual comfort.

But the most interesting if not the most amusing time I had was at one of my visits to a Turkish bath. When reclining on a couch, the proprietor came into the room, and remarked to a gentleman on the next couch, " Well, Mr. D—— the Dock Strike is not over yet." " No, sir, and never will be till that man Williams is shot," was the answer.

With reference to the above, I have very much pleasure in adding the following.

1900. On my retirement, I returned to St. Ives, and soon began to take an active interest in the public work of the town. I entered the Town Council, and became a Poor Law Guardian ; in both of these capacities I had often to consult the Local Government Board, and consequently in my many visits to London I had frequent interviews with Mr. John Burns, then President.

I wish to place on record his extreme kindness to me, and the great assistance he was at all times ready to give, especially in my endeavour to build a breakwater at Sennen Cove. The successful working of this breakwater will be referred to later.

With reference to the above extracts connected with the great London Dock Strike, to prevent any misunderstanding, I sent a proof to Mr. John Burns, and received the following reply :—

HOUSE OF COMMONS,
Nov. 9th, 1917.

DEAR COL. WILLIAMS,

Many thanks for your letter and enclosure. I pass the proof. Best wishes.

Yours sincerely,
(Signed)   JOHN BURNS.

1890. From the time I became sole manager of the Docks in 1890, there arose many points of interest, more or less connected with dock work ; for example, in 1894 the Tower Bridge was opened ; this had some effect on the shipping in the river.

1894. I was present at the cutting of the first sod at St. John's Wood, for the Great Central Railway.

On March 9th, 1899, I was again present at the opening of the line by the then President of the Board of Trade.

1897. The Blackwall Tunnel was opened in 1897 ; I was present at the opening ceremony, which was followed by a lunch, provided in the tunnel under the Thames.

1897. Queen Victoria's Diamond Jubilee took place in 1897 ; I was favoured by receiving two tickets for Buckingham Palace Gardens, from which could be seen the Royal departure and arrival.

One of my earliest friends in London is at present a prominent City solicitor. He told me that when he first commenced practice he had, like many others, a great struggle. One of his first clients was a lady, and at the conclusion of the business he asked her to have a glass of wine as it was an exceedingly hot day. She at first refused but with a little pressure she accepted on his stating it was at hand. He left the room as she thought to get the wine, when shortly after on his return, much to his surprise, the door opened and the office boy put his head just inside and said, " If you please, sir, they have no shilling bottles, the lowest is eighteen pence."

In speaking of sermons there is one I must mention which was delivered at a town that in my early years I was well acquainted with. At that time the town was undergoing many vicissitudes, business firms frequently changed, but with it all the people were fond of going to hear good sermons.

One day an eminent Scotch Doctor of Divinity was advertised to preach, consequently the chapel was crowded. I did not go although I know the chapel well.

I may say that the Doctor was a stranger to the town.

However, he took for his text, " Owe no man anything," and after directing the congregation generally to his subject, he mentioned that once a man came to him and said, " Doctor, I have retired from business, and I wish to do something for the Lord." The divine said, " Have you ever been a bankrupt ? " He answered, " Yes, many years ago." " How much did you pay ? "

"Twelve shillings and sixpence in the pound." "Have you ever since offered to pay the other seven shillings and sixpence ? " " No, because the Court passed me clear." The doctor said, " You may take it from me the Lord will never accept your services till you have paid the seven shillings and sixpence."

On leaving the building one said to another, " Who could have told the doctor about us ? "

I may say that town to-day is one of the most prosperous in the kingdom.

Whilst Mayor of St. Ives, to which I have previously referred, there were the usual annual banquets, and at one of them one of the councillors made an excellent *lapsus linguæ*.

A gentleman present, in the course of an excellent speech, made reference to Ireland, and said one of the difficult positions of that country was in consequence of so many absentee landlords.

The councillor, in his remarks which followed, said that Ireland was not alone, but that St. Ives *was infested with absentee landlords.*

Another rather peculiar sermon I remember. The minister was a most estimable man, " since gone to his rest."

One Sunday morning he took his text from Jeremiah and, after quoting the passage, said, " My friends, this book of Jeremiah puzzles me ; I don't understand it, and it is therefore quite impossible for you to do so."

One of my directors was a most estimable old gentleman, a shipowner and retired captain of the mercantile marine.

One day we were examining samples of rope, which were specially required to be of the very best quality for pier-head use.

As was usual, we were arranging to send the samples to be tested, when the captain entered the room, and seeing what was decided on, asked if I would oblige him by having a sample at his office also tested. I agreed, and he went and returned with a long length of small rope.

Seeing he was much disturbed, I asked the cause. He said, " On the way a gentleman in passing said, ' Don't be in any hurry, Captain, the State will do it for you in good time.' "

Speaking of rope, there is a case I must mention. Although it took place some time ago it is still fresh in my memory, and it illustrates how at times some of the best commercial men are deceived.

There was at that time in London a noted firm of rope manufacturers. One morning a " gentleman " called on the principal and said, he had just completed a contract with one of the largest shipowners for the construction of two large steamers. The owner had specially stipulated that the rope furnished was to come from his firm, and that his father had requested him to visit the works. The principal replied, " Certainly, but it is lunch time, we will have lunch." Afterwards the works were visited, and whilst there an invitation was given for dinner and a visit to the theatre. The " gentleman " said he was unable to accept the invitation, having to return that evening, and that he was unprovided with funds. He was then offered £10, which was accepted at once.

The next morning the manufacturer went to the shipowner to thank him, and to his surprise was told it was all false, as he had never seen or heard of the visitor. I said to the manufacturer when he told me the tale, " Why were you so taken in ? " He replied, " My dear sir, I was so struck with his story that I would have given him fifty pounds if he had asked for it."

1894. There was war in 1894 between China

and Japan. Just after the declaration of peace there arrived in this country from China Li Hung Chang, described as Chinese Ambassador and Grand Secretary.

As he was desirous of seeing the river and its shipping, I was asked by the Embassy to take him down to the Docks, and I was also requested by several City firms to allow some of their representatives to accompany us, as they anticipated orders from China.

On the way down he certainly was very inquisitive about my home and family, etc.

At the Docks at that time there was a Japanese battleship being fitted out, so I asked through the interpreter if he would like to go on board ; but the invitation was, however, declined with a strong shake of the head. I never heard that any firm ever received an order from his Excellency ; all I got was his signature which took up one page of my autograph book. I might also add amongst other questions, he asked how many directors I had ; on being told he coolly remarked, " Too many cooks spoil the broth."

In addition to the general management of the Docks, I had on many occasions to make arrangements for the reception of Royal visitors at the Docks. I do not think there was a single member of our Royal Family whom at some time or other I had not the pleasure of either accompanying or receiving at the Docks. Often several of the Royal Family came together.

I have also had the honour of conducting over the Docks many foreign kings and queens, amongst whom were the late King and Queen of Denmark, and the present King ; the late King of Sweden, the King and Queen of Würtemberg, and the late King of Rumania. Shortly after the visit of the King of Rumania I received the following letter :—

SIR,   LONDON, *July 5th*, 1892.

By command of His Majesty the King, I beg to forward to you a medal, which was coined in Rumania last year, to celebrate the 25th Anniversary of His Majesty's Accession to the Throne, and which His Majesty desires you to keep as a memento of his visit to the Docks.

I remain, sir,
Yours faithfully,
(Signed)   A. P. PLANYE.

H. W. Williams, Esq.

Returning to the visits of members of our Royal Family to the Docks, it would occupy too much space to describe in detail all of them ; but, fortunately for me, I am in possession of most of their autographs in my book.

1887. One of the earliest, and I am sure one of the most interesting, was a visit from our present King.

In 1887 the Governors of the Greenwich Seamen's Hospital asked the Docks Company for a site in the Royal Albert Dock for erecting a small branch of their hospital, to meet the needs of the seamen using the Dock. The request was of course readily granted ; the foundation stone was laid by King George (then Prince George of Wales), and the institution was formally opened on July 24th, 1890, by the Prince and Princess of Wales, afterwards King Edward VII and Queen Alexandra.

That little hospital has since grown into a very large one, the number of beds having increased from twelve to fifty, and a thriving Tropical

School has been added, which was attended before the war by nearly two hundred students, all fully qualified men. At the hospital no less than twenty thousand patients are treated now during a year.

1892. Another case I must mention, that of the sad death of H.R.H. Prince Albert Victor, the Duke of Clarence, on the 14th January, 1892.

I remember one Sunday going to the Royal Albert Docks to receive His Royal Highness on his return from Gibraltar. On asking him how he proposed getting to town, his equerry said " H.R.H. expected a carriage to have met him." I told him the carriage might possibly be at Liverpool Street Station, from which we were seven miles ; that I had a special train, and I would be very pleased if H.R.H. would join me. He did so, but on arrival at Liverpool Street Station there was no carriage ; so a cab was called. I do not forget the look of the driver when told to drive to Marlborough House.

The large shipping companies, using the Docks, frequently added to their fleet of steamers ; and it was the usual custom when a new steamer was ready for sea, for the owners to invite shippers, etc. to inspect the vessel. This was generally followed by a lunch on board, at which speeches were made in praise of the steamer *Manora*.

At one lunch as usual the speakers expressed themselves as delighted with the ship, when a call was made for a speech from the Commander.

He said, " I have heard all of you speak in praise of my vessel, but I expect if any one of you could get quoted 10d. per ton less freight you would forget the *Manora*."

1901. Queen Victoria passed away after a long and most eventful reign in January, 1901. As before mentioned, I saw when a child a display of fireworks on the occasion of her Coronation, and I was present at Paddington Station, and there witnessed the departure of the cortège and Royal Family for the interment at Windsor.

On January 20th, 1901, the Prince of Wales succeeded to the throne as King Edward VII, and was crowned at Westminster Abbey, August 9th, 1902.

There is one important matter I should not fail to mention; one, which from a very small beginning, became of considerable value to the community at large.

I refer to the frozen meat trade. I believe the first refrigerating chamber in London was erected at the Royal Victoria Dock, and was of small dimensions, being capable only of containing 10,000 carcases of sheep.

At the time of my retirement, accommodation was provided for 250,000, and, as the importations began to increase, additional accommodation had to be found, both at the West India Dock and at the Smithfield Market for 100,000 each. Eventually, the four stores were capable of holding over 500,000. In addition to sheep and lambs, mention must be made of the large importations of beef and rabbits.

1899. In concluding my very imperfect and superficial remarks on the management of a vast undertaking like the Docks, it is evident that to give full particulars would occupy volumes; but, in order to give some idea of the extent, I will mention a few of the items spent in my last year.

Wages of workmen £567,220. This was only one half of the amount spent before the ship-owners undertook their own discharge.

Salaries £122,422, upkeep £110,000, dredging

£30,168, rates and taxes £92,364, coals and coke £36,359.

On the day previous to my departure I had an interview with Sir Alexander Binnie, then Engineer to the London County Council (since deceased). We were discussing and settling the final touches of the Rotherhithe Tunnel, since completed. He said, " Where are you going ? " I replied, " To my native Cornwall." " Whatever will you do there after your long and strenuous life here. However, take my advice, when down there, don't lean against a wall."

Well, I have not forgotten Sir Alexander's parting words, as a further perusal of these recollections plainly shows.

1900. I finally add that on leaving the Directors, together with the Staff, invited me to a dinner on the 17th November, 1900, at which I was presented with three silver salvers.

Just before my retirement I received from His Majesty a Commission as Lieut.-Colonel in the Engineer and Railway Staff Corps, also a commission as Justice of the Peace for the County of Middlesex.

1901. I returned to Cornwall in 1901 to reside, and in 1903 I also received a Commission as a Justice of the Peace for the County of Cornwall.

1905. One of my first important public duties in Cornwall was in 1905. I was called upon to preside at a Board of Trade enquiry into the very serious wreck, when near the Land's End in a violent gale, of the full-rigged sailing ship *Khyber* of Liverpool, on her passage from Australia to Queenstown, on the 15th February, when twenty-three out of her crew of twenty-six were drowned.

The Court of Enquiry was composed of an admiral, a naval commander, a mercantile com-

F

mander, and four county magistrates, and the enquiry was considered of great importance, as a question had arisen as to the coast guard patrol on the night of the wreck.

So great was the force of the gale that it was found impossible to launch the Sennen life-boat.

Sennen Cove was the only spot in which a lifeboat could be placed between St. Ives and Penzance, for serving forty-five miles of the most dangerous sea coast in England, and even there it was in an opening amongst the rocks.

Failing the launching of the lifeboat, every effort was made by the whole of the inhabitants of the cove to get the rocket apparatus to the wreck, but before its arrival the ship went to pieces, and within fifteen minutes scarcely a vestige of the vessel was to be seen.

At the enquiry a strong desire was felt that if possible some steps should be taken to remedy the existing state of things.

(1) In the interest of lifeboat work and shipping.

(2) In the interest of the fishermen who man the lifeboat.

(3) To enable the lifeboat to be launched at any state of tide or weather.

I therefore made an appeal first to the Treasury, and afterwards to the public generally ; from the Treasury I received £1300, and from all sources over £5000.

At considerable trouble and expense I promoted a Provisional Order, and received the Royal Assent on the 9th August, 1907.

It is impossible for me to speak too highly of the kindness and assistance I received from the Treasury, Board of Trade, Lifeboat Institution, Land Owners, Trinity House, and particularly from the Duchy of Cornwall, through H.R.H. the Prince of Wales, now His Majesty King George V.

1908. Amidst great rejoicing in July, 1908, the memorial stone was laid, and the breakwater is now virtually complete.

I was the recipient of numerous letters of congratulation, all of which I value ; but perhaps the letter I appreciate most is one I had from the Prince of Wales (our present King). The following is a copy :—

1909. DUCHY OF CORNWALL OFFICE,
BUCKINGHAM GATE, S.W.,
April 1st, 1909.

DEAR COLONEL WILLIAMS,

The Prince of Wales has been pleased to sanction a further donation of £100, from the Duchy revenue, towards the Sennen Cove Breakwater and Harbour.

His Royal Highness was very pleased at the success which has attended your untiring efforts for this much-needed harbour, and at the splendid way the fishermen and others have responded to the appeal.

I am,
Yours truly,
(Signed)   WALTER PEACOCK.

My action with regard to the necessity of building a breakwater at Sennen Cove has been fully justified on several occasions ; for shortly after its erection the full-rigged ship *Fairport*, of Liverpool, was in distress, and the Press at that time bore witness to the speedy launching of the lifeboat in the teeth of a terrific gale—a feat hitherto quite impossible. Both the ship and crew were saved.

I would also mention that at the wreck enquiry

the Court made the following important recommendations :—

(1) That each man on patrol should be furnished with a small pair of marine glasses and a suitable lamp.

(2) That the dangerous parts of the coastguard's paths in close proximity to the cliffs should be more distinctly marked.

(3) That some improved method of communication between the mainland and adjacent light-ships and lighthouses should be provided.

BOARD OF TRADE ENQUIRY *re* " KHYBER "

[*Extract from " The Western Morning News," May 30th,* 1905.]

" The Chairman, after delivering judgment, said as the enquiry was now closed the Magistrates and Assessors would send in a report containing some observations and suggestions respecting the patrolling of the coast, and also the connecting of the lighthouses. They desired to bear their unanimous testimony to how well all the witnesses gave their evidence, and the satisfaction they felt for the way in which everyone tried his hardest to render assistance. They desired particularly to mention the Sennen lifeboat men, who, finding they could not launch their lifeboat, helped the coastguards to get the rocket apparatus out, and hauled it a considerable distance up a tremendous hill to meet the horses. Their conduct was most praiseworthy. He was requested to say that the Court expressed its extreme sympathy with the relatives of the unfortunate people who were lost in the *Khyber*. He did not think anyone could possibly imagine the anguish and suffering they endured on that fateful night."

1908. The memorial stone of the breakwater bears the following inscription :—

" This stone was placed here by the Fisher-men of the Cove, to remind future generations that this Breakwater was built by public sub-scriptions, raised by the untiring efforts of Colonel Williams, J.P., of St. Ives, to whom and to all subscribers the Covers owe a great debt of gratitude. July, 1908."

My remarks respecting Sennen Cove apply, of course, more particularly to the fishermen now engaged in fishing there ; but I am confident that when the younger fishermen, now serving in the Navy and elsewhere, return to their normal calling after the war, they will understand and appreciate what has been done on their behalf, with respect to the improvement of their harbour, and, more-over, that the object of the Stone — to remind future generations—will not be lost sight of by them.

In addition to my magisterial duties in Corn-wall, sitting frequently on three and four Benches, I became in an unguarded moment a member of the Penzance Board of Guardians, also a member of the St. Ives Town Council, a Commissioner of Income Tax, a member of the Cornwall Sea Fisheries, a member of the Cornwall County Licens-ing Committee, and a School Board Manager.

I have no hesitation in stating that in sitting on the two former bodies I found it was vastly different from presiding over a large number of some of the principal commercial gentlemen in the City of London.

In the deliberations of both of these bodies there was a certain (as they say in sporting par-lance) "run-as-you-please" style of procedure.

I think most of the Guardians were farmers. On my joining the Board, I brought forward four important matters for the consideration of the Board :—

(1) Standing Orders for the better conduct of the business.

(2) Telephone communication between the Workhouse and Police Station in case of fire.

(3) A night nurse to be in attendance on the aged and infirm patients.

(4) The advisability and necessity of giving dental attention to the children.

I tried, with regard to the first matter, to point out to them what valuable time would be saved, and mentioned other advantages, but they were at a loss to understand it. Had Standing Orders been adopted many of their speeches, much to their regret, would not have appeared in the local papers.

One gentleman present said to me, " Why raise such a question as Standing Orders ? Some are continually standing."

As to number two, the Workhouse, situated some two and a half miles from Penzance, had a large number of aged and infirm people as inmates and only one or two able-bodied men available in case of fire.

I suggested having telephonic communication ; at that time I think the only one in Penzance was at the Police Station, whereas to-day there are over one hundred. My recommendation was most strenuously opposed ; they never had a fire, and it was a waste of money. However, I eventually succeeded, and I am assured that, leaving out the fire question, the telephone has been found extremely useful.

Respecting the third matter, the necessity of a night nurse was also vehemently opposed, as members failed to see that the dictionary defined a guardian as a protector of the old and infirm, and not as a protector of the rates.

Since I retired as a member of the Board of Guardians, I have followed in the local press with much interest the proceedings at the Board meetings, particularly as regards the night-nurse question, and was glad to read that my original suggestion has been agreed to.

One day in London I called as usual at the Local Government Board Office, and had an interview with Mr. John Burns (then President).

On my return to St. Ives I was highly amused at receiving through their clerk an official letter from the Penzance Board of Guardians stating that great surprise was felt at my visiting the Local Government Board without their authority, and adding that such a thing was quite unprecedented. Of course the effect on me was nil, except that I sympathised with them on the narrow view they had taken. In my reply I told them that I had in a prominent position hanging in my room a motto, which for many years had guided me. It says :—

" I shall pass through this world but once. If, therefore, there be any kindness I can show, or any good thing I can do, let me do it now ; for I shall not pass this way again."

However, one of the results of my interview with Mr. John Burns was, that a Lady Inspector was sent down, and I know she made a strong report on the necessity of a night nurse.

As to number four, the advisability of dental attention for the children, the Guardians declined to entertain such a suggestion ; yet it has been found by the War Department that a very large number of recruits was considered unsatisfactory because of their defective teeth, and the Authorities have deemed it necessary to add a considerable number of dentists to the service. At a recent Inspection at Aldershot some 75 per cent of the troops were in need of dental treatment.

On becoming a member of the St. Ives Town Council, I found in my opinion some few irregularities in the proceedings ; but I wish to state distinctly that, in any remarks I make, I have no desire to cast the slightest reflection on the Council or on any member.

I only wish to record a few instances which arose during the proceedings.

The Council were in possession of Standing Orders and Bye-laws ; but, as to the latter, although passed and sanctioned in 1896, they had not to any extent been adhered to. One prominent case arose, and for my own satisfaction I felt it advisable to consult Mr. Macmoran, the eminent King's Counsel on Municipal Law, and on his report the scheme was withdrawn.

However, I was elected Mayor in 1910, and re-elected in 1911.

During my mayoralty, I found there was considerable misunderstanding amongst several members on various points, so in May, 1910, I issued a memorandum containing some clauses from Acts of Parliament on Municipal duties. A reprint of this memorandum may be found interesting.

For the information and guidance
of the members of the Council.

(*Note* from "Arnold's Municipal Corporations
Law")

Section 12, Sub-Sec. (c) MUNICIPAL
CORPORATIONS ACT, 1882

A person shall be disqualified, etc.

Note.—It is most important that the members
of a Council should be above suspicion. They
should have no interest to bias their judgments
in deciding what is for the public good. The
leaning of the Courts seems to be to a strict
interpretation of this sub-section. It is clear that
members of a Town Council should be advised to
keep themselves absolutely free from the possi-
bility of any imputation in this respect. The first
essential of good local self-government is purity
of administration, and to attain that object the
Courts will give full effect to this sub-section.

THE PUBLIC HEALTH ACT, 1875
Schedule 2.   Rule 64.

DISQUALIFICATION OF MEMBERS

Any member who ceases to hold his qualifica-
tion, or becomes bankrupt, or submits his affairs
to liquidation by arrangement or compounds
with his creditors, or is absent from meetings of
the local board for more than six months con-
secutively (unless in case of illness), or accepts or
holds any office or place of profit under the local
board of which he is a member or in any manner
is concerned in any bargain or contract entered
into by such board, or participates in the profit
thereof, or any work done under the authority of
this Act in or for the District, shall, except in the

cases next hereinafter provided, cease to be such member, and his office as such shall thereupon become vacant :

Provided that no member shall vacate his office—

> By reason of his being interested in the sale or lease of any lands or in any loan of money to the local board ; or

> By reason of his being interested in any contract with the local board as a shareholder in any joint stock company ; but he shall not vote at any meeting of the local board on any question in which such company are interested, save that in the case of a water company, or other company established for the carrying on of works of a like public nature, this prohibition may be dispensed with by the Local Government Board.

MUNICIPAL CORPORATIONS ACT, 1882

Section 12.—A person shall be disqualified for being elected and for being a Councillor, if and while he has, directly or indirectly, by himself or his partner, any share or interest in any Contract or employment with, by, or on behalf of, the Council (except any Lease or sale of Lands, etc., or agreement for loan of money, etc., or Newspaper, or Company which Contracts for Lighting, Water Supply, or Fire Insurance, or Railway Company, or Incorporated Company, etc.).

Section 22, *Sub-Section* 3.—A member of the Council shall not vote or take part in the discussion of any matter before the Council, or a Committee, in which he has, directly or indirectly, by himself or by his partner, any pecuniary interest.

Section 41.—If any person acts in a Corporate office after becoming disqualified he shall for each offence be liable to a fine not exceeding £50 recoverable by action (brought by a Burgess).

Note.—If any Builder or other Person presents a Plan to the Council for the erection of a Building, the making of a Road, or for any other purpose, and such is not in accordance with the existing Bye-laws, and consequently returned, and if such Builder or Person does commence to erect he comes under Bye-law 98 which says, " He shall be liable for every such offence to the penalty of £5 and a further sum of 40s. per day after written notice."

If any Builder or other Person presents a Plan to the Council for the erection of a Building, making of a Road, or for any other purpose not in accordance with the existing Bye-laws, and if inadvertently or otherwise the Council pass such Plan an Action may be instituted by any Rate-payer as there is no defence to it.

See Attorney-General *v.* Ashton Recreation Ground Co.

The remedy is against the Builder or Person and not against the Council, though they acted illegally in approving the Plan in defiance of their own Bye-laws, but this in no way protects the Builder.

There were other questions I brought forward for consideration, such as workmen's dwellings, division of the town into wards, and the provision of municipal buildings. It will be remembered that the late Sir Edward Hain offered a site for such buildings which was refused.

To me that refusal was most unfortunate, for I believe had the offer been accepted, ways and means would have been found for the erection of a building worthy of our dear old town without becoming a heavy burden on the shoulders of the public.

The continual point raised was economy. I recollect one eminent man saying, "One hears a good deal of the evils of reckless extravagance, but I am sometimes inclined to think that the effects of reckless economy may be just as disastrous."

In 1908 I attended the King's Levee, and was presented by the Inspector-General of the Forces. I also attended in June 1909 and 1913.

During my two years of mayoralty, there took place many public and other very interesting events, the most important being the death of King Edward VII in May, 1910, and the accession of His Majesty King George V, and the latter's Coronation on 22nd June, 1911. It is almost, needless to say that the Coronation was celebrated at St. Ives in a most loyal manner.

As Mayor, I sent on behalf of the borough a telegram of congratulation to His Majesty, and received the following :—

BUCKINGHAM PALACE.

The Mayor, St. Ives, Cornwall.

I am commanded by the King to ask you to express to the inhabitants of St. Ives His Majesty's sincere thanks for their telegram of congratulations and expressions of loyalty.

(Signed)   A. BIGGS.

1911. In addition to the above telegram, I received the following from the Home Secretary.

HOME OFFICE, WHITEHALL,
July 28th, 1911.

SIR,

I have received the King's commands to transmit to you the accompanying medal, which His Majesty has been graciously pleased to confer upon you, to be worn in remembrance of the Coronation of Their Majesties.

I have to request that you will be good enough to send me an acknowledgment of the receipt of the medal.

I am, sir,
Your obedient Servant,
(Signed)   WINSTON S. CHURCHILL.

The Mayor,
  St. Ives, Cornwall.

CHAPTER VI

1911. There is another important point of considerable interest to which I must refer.

As a member of the Cornwall Sea Fisheries Committee, I have taken great interest in the Cornwall Fishing Industry.

At an annual meeting of Representatives and Authorities, held at the House of Lords' Committee Room on the 9th July, 1911, I specially called attention to the disastrous state of the fishing industry in West Cornwall at that time.

Lord Carrington, President of the Board, was in the chair. I cannot do better than quote from the Government Report of the meeting, which gives my remarks on the subject.

Colonel Williams (Cornwall): In your opening remarks, my Lord, you stated that the fishing industry was in a very flourishing condition.

The Chairman: I hope so.

Colonel Williams: I am sorry to differ from your Lordship as far as I, personally, am concerned. Although I am the representative of Cornwall, I also represent St. Ives in Cornwall, which is a fishing town, and the fishing season has been most disastrous. Therefore I want to ask whether it is not possible that something can be done. We have with us something like 500 fishermen, and I have always considered that the fishing industry is more or less a nursery for those who supply the Navy, which is our great protection. I find we have there alone 250 Naval Reserve men, 90 of whom are in possession of long-service medals. That shows that their interest at all events is in the Navy eventually ; but the fishing industry had been so bad of late that many of the men are not earning bread, and the consequence is that they have to go to the mines. What I am asking you to do is this. I do not know whether it comes under this head of the Agenda or not. Is it not possible that some help from the Government in some shape or form can be given to those men to help them to continue to live, because they are only existing, they are not living at the present time ?

The Chairman : What sort of fishermen are they ?

Colonel Williams : Good ones.

The Chairman : Line fishermen ?

Colonel Williams : All-round thorough good ones.

The Chairman : Are they line fishermen ?

Colonel Williams : No, drift luggers, a few trawlers and long-liners. I know, my Lord, it is treading on dangerous ground, but when I look at the report of the Cousul-General of Germany which I have in my hand and see what Germany is doing for its fishermen, I must say it makes my heart bleed to think of it. He says here : " The herring-fishing companies receive a subvention of £300 towards the building of each sailing vessel known as luggers, and £100 for outfit, while for the building of the smaller vessels, of owners' smacks, the Government lends money on easy terms, no repayments being required for the first two or three years. Steam fishing vessels are not entitled to these benefits "—we have no steam—

"but those engaged in the herring trade in common with the sailing craft participate in a reserve fund out of which losses in nets and gear are made up and the German herring fishery is thus strongly protected." I ask, my Lord, cannot something be done in our unfortunate case. I believe there are other towns such as Newlyn and Mousehole which are almost in the same position. The consequence is the men are leaving for abroad because they cannot live at home. Therefore I cannot congratulate you in stating that the fishing industry is a flourishing industry at present because there is an exception in my case.

The Chairman : Will you make some proposal so that we can get to some business and we will take the sense of the meeting ? Will you propose that a subvention should be made by the Government to help people to build boats at St. Ives ? If you will do that I will take the sense of the meeting.

Colonel Williams : All I am asking is this, I do not know how to put it, I should be very glad to consider any suggestion your Lordship makes. I am not in a position at present to make any proposal. I am throwing this out to show the present state of the fishing industry in the West Country.

Mr. M. Dunn (Cornwall) : If I should be in order, I am prepared to substantiate at least in some form the statement which has fallen from Colonel Williams.

Fortunately, I was very strongly supported at the meeting by several representatives, and, as a result, the Government appointed a special Commission to visit the Cornish fishing ports.

Eventually, the Development Board advanced a loan of £4000 to enable the fishermen of West Cornwall to instal motors in their boats.

The advancement of the money has been amply justified, the whole experiment having proved eminently satisfactory. Not long ago the Chairman of the Development Board sent me a letter of congratulation on its success.

I have every reason to believe that the Government has decided to make further grants in the same direction.

In connection with the success mentioned, although on account of the war a large number of West Cornwall fishermen are serving in the Navy, many boats are idle; yet I find there are in Newlyn 27, Mousehole 29, Porthleven 50, and in St. Ives 49 boats with motors installed.

I have previously stated what I did for the fishermen of Sennen Cove in providing them with a breakwater; it is therefore with extreme regret that I am inserting a copy of a memorandum I made at the time (October 28th, 1914). The memorandum speaks for itself.

1914.

October 28th, 1914.

Memorandum as to the present position of Sennen Cove in relation to Col. Williams' correspondence with the Development Board.

————

On Monday the 19th inst. Colonel Williams, accompanied by Colonel Cornish and Mr. Lewis, Engineer, visited the Cove and called a meeting of the fishermen. He told them that for some years he had in numerous visits to London urged the Board to give some further pecuniary assist-

G

ance to complete the harbour by two necessary objects, viz. :—

1. To remove the rocks at the entrance, thus making it safer for fishing - boats and facilitating the working of the lifeboat at low water.

2. To make a road or slip to enable carts to go down for coals, salt, bricks, seaweed, etc., etc.

3. Further protection against the encroachment of the sea at the western shore end of the breakwater.

The rocks if removed would accomplish Nos. 2 and 3.

In this he was not successful.

But, in consequence of the war breaking out and a general falling off in fishing, and a desire on the part of the Government that measures should be taken to relieve any distress arising therefrom, he had made fresh representation to the Board to the effect that at Sennen there was a large number of fishermen earning little, and if a Grant were made, he would endeavour to get the above works done on a co-operative principle by engaging the fishermen themselves and thus enable them and their families to tide over the winter.

On this the Development Board made the following offer, viz :—

(1) A Grant of £100, on condition that another £100 was obtained locally.

(2) A loan of £300 for 50 years at 4 per cent.

He said he had given his personal guarantee for the second £100, and that the present financial position of the harbour was thus :—

The present debt due to the Bank was £185 ;

there was in hand £28 15s., leaving a balance of £156 5s. As to the credit side, the dues were about £17 per annum and the rent of a house £32 ; total annual earnings about £49.

The interest on the bank debt is £7 10s. and the interest and annual payments on the proposed loan of £300, for fifty years would be about £14. Total £21 10s. against earnings £49. Both Col. Cornish and Mr. Lewis spoke to the fishermen and urged them for the various reasons mentioned, to at once accept the offer, but when put to them they declined to agree to it. They were unable to give any satisfactory reason beyond that they were binding themselves to a debt of £300 for fifty years and would not consider the advantages to be derived from it.

I also told them that if the proposed work was accomplished, I was satisfied there was every prospect of getting a motor lifeboat at Sennen Cove.

Col. Williams told them in consequence of their action that day, his connection with Sennen Cove now ceased.

During the two years of my mayoralty there were several matters of considerable local interest, of which I will mention five.

1910. (1) The inauguration of the new Water Works.

(2) The presentation of the Freedom of the Borough to Sir Edward Hain.

1911. (3) The Coronation of His Majesty George V.

1910. (4) The visit of the Royal Cornwall Agricultural Show to St. Ives.

1911. (5) The Knill Steeple ceremony.

The inauguration of the Water Works took

place on Easter Monday, 1910. The reservoir, situated at Bussow Moors, near Halsetown, was constructed at a cost of about £15,000. The formal opening of such a reservoir being of great importance locally, I cannot do better than quote a few extracts from the Press :—

" At 2.15 p.m. a large company assembled at the Council Chamber and, headed by the local Territorial Band, proceeded to the new Water Works. Those present included His Worship the Mayor (Colonel Williams, J.P.), accompanied by the Mayoress, and his Chaplain (the Rev. S. F. Marsh, Vicar of St. Ives), the Mayor and Mayoress of Penzance (Mr. and Mrs. A. K. Barnett), Aldermen R. S. Read, J.P., J. Daniel, J.P., T. Row Harry, J.P., Councillors J. Pearce (ex-Mayor), W. Faull, J.P., W. Blight, J.P., J. Ninnis, G. Williams, J. Stevens and J. Daniel, jun. ; Messrs. Edward Boase (Town Clerk), Reginald Boase (Deputy Town Clerk), A. P. I. Cotterell, C.E., Bristol (the engineer who designed the works), Arthur Carkeek, Redruth (the contractor), F. E. Wintle (Borough Surveyor), Albert E. Brookes (County Surveyor), W. Hearson (Gas Manager), T. J. Chellew (representing the St. Ives Consolidated Mines, Ltd.), Revs. W. Whittley (Vicar of Towednack), R. E. Griffin, M.A. (Vicar of Halsetown), G. B. Kirby (Zion Church), and A. Johnson (Primitive Methodist), Messrs. W. Trewhella, J.P., L. E. Comley, J.P., W. G. Hancock, T. Millie Dow, Commander J. Chellew, R.N.R., Dr. Matthew, and several ladies.
The Mayor and Corporation were accommodated on a temporary platform near the commemoration-stone, and in the proximity of this

quite a large crowd gathered, and with the weather of an ideal nature, the conditions were very pleasant.

The Mayor said he thought it was right and proper that they should commence the proceedings by thanking God for giving them such a glorious day, also to thank Him for what He had enabled them to accomplish for the welfare of the town, and to ask His blessing on the work they were about to inaugurate. [Hear, hear.] His Worship then asked his Chaplain to conduct the brief religious ceremony, which opened with the recital of the Lord's Prayer, followed by other prayers, and then the reading of the appropriate lesson from St. John iv. 5–14. The singing of the Old Hundredth (which was heartily joined in by 'One and All') and the pronouncement of the Benediction concluded this part of the ceremony.

In requesting Mrs. Read to open the reservoir, the Mayor spoke of the important part Alderman Read had played in procuring the reservoir. No one knew the trouble Mr. Read had taken, the time he had spent over it, the worry he had had, and the sleepless nights he had spent in order that that work might be brought to a satisfactory conclusion. [Hear, hear.] 'It is fitting, therefore,' added the Mayor, 'that Mrs. Read should perform this ceremony.' [Applause.]

Mrs. Read then opened the reservoir by releasing the valve, Mr. Carkeek presenting her with a gold key with which to unlock the chain. A fountain below the reservoir at once came into play, amidst cheers, showing that an effective pressure was obtainable. The Union Jack was hoisted, and the Band played 'God bless the Prince of Wales.' Mrs. Read having performed the task set her, said : ' I have much pleasure in releasing the valve, and I hope this supply of water may be sufficient for St. Ives for many years to come.' [Applause.]

A dainty little presentation trowel having been given her by the engineer, the Mayoress, amidst applause, declared the commemoration-stone to be ' well and truly laid.'

The inscription on the stone is :—' St. Ives Reservoir. Commenced 1908, J. Pearce, Mayor ; inaugurated 1910, H. W. Williams. J.P., Mayor ; Alderman Read, J.P., Chairman ; Alderman Harry, J.P., Alderman Daniel, J.P., Councillor Faull, J.P. ; Edward Boase (town clerk), A. Carkeek (contractor), A. P. I. Cotterell (engineer), F. E. Wintle (surveyor).'

Councillor Pearce, in proposing thanks to the Mayoress and Mrs. Read, said he thought the new Water Works formed one of the most valuable assets of the town. They had a supply which would be unfailing and absolutely pure.

The compliment was cordially awarded, and the Mayor acknowledged it for the ladies, remarking that he was delighted to see that work there, as he was deeply interested in the welfare of his native town.

The party then adjourned to the filter-house, where Mr. Wintle, the Borough Surveyor, explained the working and exhibited the drawings of the buildings and plant.

The Mayor and Mayoress were afterwards ' At Home ' to a large number of guests at Mr. Husband's farm (near the filter-house at Consols), where afternoon tea was served."

1910. When I brought the question of conferring the Freedom of the Borough on Sir Edward Hain before the Council, it was at once unanimously agreed to, as the members were only too delighted that the first Freedom of the Borough of St. Ives should be presented to Sir Edward, not only on account of the very many valuable services he had rendered to his native town, but also in appreciation of the honour of knighthood recently conferred on him.

1911. The celebration on June 22nd, 1911, of the Coronations of His Majesty George V and Queen Mary, was, as stated before, observed at St. Ives with great loyalty.

The visit of the Royal Cornwall Show to St. Ives in 1910 was eminently satisfactory, as may be gathered from the Annual Report of the Society.

1911. As full details of the Knill Steeple Ceremony have often appeared in the public press, there is no need for me to refer to the festivities.

1915. In January, 1915, my attention was called in several ways, such as by the " Western Morning News," the Penzance Navy League, and Colonel Cornish, Penzance, as to the necessity of better coast watching on the Cornish coast, but more particularly so by a very interesting circular issued by Colonel Cornish, in which he specially pointed out, that the numerous coves around the Cornish coast were unprotected, and that there was a strong feeling in favour of the suggestion that as hostile submarines were cruising in that district, they would avail themselves of the secrecy of the coves.

Arising therefrom public meetings were held at Penzance (at which I presided) and strong resolutions were passed, urging the Admiralty to take some action.

I called at the Admiralty, and eventually received the following :—

ADMIRALTY, S.W.,
13th March, 1915.

SIR,

With reference to your letter of the 22nd ultimo, addressed to the Additional Civil Lord, on the subject of Coast Watching in Cornwall, I am commanded by My Lords Commissioners of the Admiralty to acquaint you that the scheme of coast watching adopted has been very carefully gone into by the District Captain of Coast Guard, Bristol, who has organised a system which their Lordships consider will be quite effective.

Provision is made in the scheme for utilising the assistance of civilian watchers who will act as deputy to the officer in charge of coast watching.

The District Captain reports that the deputies have already been of the greatest assistance to him.

I am, sir,
Your obedient servant,
(Signed)   O. MURRAY.

Colonel H. W. Williams,
St. Ives, Cornwall.

CHAPTER VII

DURING the many years I was absent from Cornwall, I never failed when an opportunity arose of speaking of its natural beauties, and as a health resort. At the same time it cannot be denied there are other places with similar claims.

Many years ago, one summer's evening I was sitting by the side of the river Derwent, near Matlock, and getting into conversation with an elderly gentleman, the question of the health of the district arose.

He said, "I think you will be surprised, sir, when I tell you there is not a resident doctor within three miles from where we are now sitting. I replied that it certainly spoke well for the district.

He also said, here it was said that at one time a young doctor came down from one of the London hospitals, he had an interview with an old gentleman resident, whom he asked if he thought there was an opening for a medical man. The old gentleman asked, "What is a medical man?" He answered, "One to cure disease." "But there is no disease." The young man asked, "But don't people die here?" "Oh, yes, but in rotation; I am fourth to go now."

1917. I have previously referred to the difficulty I experienced during my mayoralty in getting the St. Ives Town Council to adhere to their own bye-laws.

At the time of writing, circumstances seem to point out that no improvement has taken place.

A short time ago the St. Ives fishermen asked me to take up the question of improving the mode of selling their fish.

A public meeting was called to which all parties interested were invited : fishermen, salesmen, and buyers were present ; the whole question was fully discussed, and certain resolutions were unanimously agreed to.

1917. Accordingly I went to the Board of Trade, furnished with the resolutions, which I requested should be made into bye-laws.

This was done and the bye-laws sent to the Council. In the meantime the Harbour Committee made a recommendation to the Council, that there should be an addition made to the bye-laws, in connection with the disposal of fish offal. The recommendation was approved also, and passed by the Council, sanctioned by the Board of Trade, and advertised in the usual way, all plain sailing without a word of opposition from any one ; then signed and sealed.

But, when a flagrant case recently arose that demanded prompt action on the part of the Authority, a determined stand was made, not only by some members of the Harbour Committee, but also by other members of the Council, not to enforce the very bye-laws they had themselves framed.

I feel I should be remiss if I did not take this opportunity of inserting something with reference to a matter of an important character in connection with St. Ives.

I refer to the old question of a harbour of refuge ; a question that has been before us ever since I can remember.

However, it is known by many that in 1904 the Joint Committee of the Devon and Cornwall County Councils instructed Mr. William Matthews Snow Sir William) the eminent engineer, to report as to the best position and construction of a harbour of refuge on the north coast of Cornwall or Devon.

Sir William did accordingly, and furnished a report dated June 24th, 1906.

It is needless for me to say that the report was most interesting and instructive reading.

I may here mention that, whilst residing in London, I attended once or twice deputations to the President of the Board of Trade (the late Mr. Joseph Chamberlain), and I have a strong recollection that at that time he laid great stress on the fact that sailing ships were decreasing, steamers taking their place ; and that therefore the necessity for a harbour of refuge was declining.

However, returning to Sir William's report, he has pointed out that as far back as 1858, a Select Committee recommended an expenditure of £174,000 for the construction of a breakwater of 2000 feet in length, a sum manifestly inadequate for the work.

Again the Royal Commission of 1859 stated their belief that the claims of St. Ives were paramount to all others, and recommended the expenditure of £400,000 for the construction of a breakwater of 3750 feet. Then came the Select Committee of 1884 which did not determine between the relative advantages of the ports, that had been brought to their notice. The only place, however, which they mentioned favourably on the north coast of Cornwall was St. Ives.

Again in April, 1904, Commander Frederick, R.N., made a report to the Board of Trade, to which he added an analysis of the list of casualties which might possibly have been averted, if a harbour of refuge had existed in the vicinity.

In 1906 I attended a public meeting held at St. Ives, presided over by Mr. Pendarves, at which Sir William went fully into the whole question.

It will therefore be seen that every committee and commission in their conclusions, decided that St. Ives was the best position, and Sir William in his excellent report, after numerous references, finished as follows, " Again there is the further argument in favour of St. Ives, viz. the prevalence of wrecks there, as shown by Commander Frederick's memorandum. I consider therefore, on the whole, that St. Ives is the preferable position for a National Harbour of Refuge."

Early in 1913 I was advised that application had been made to the Board of Trade for permission to dredge for tin in St. Ives Bay, I proceeded to London to get the facts. I at once saw that if permission was granted, it would seriously affect the St. Ives Herring Fishery, I returned home with a fixed determination to oppose it at all costs. It would not be possible to go fully into the correspondence, the several public meetings held, and the resolutions passed against the proposal.

Eventually I got the Boards of Trade and Fisheries to hold an enquiry, which was held on 12th December, 1913, and was presided over by Mr. C. E. Fryer (now Sir Charles Fryer) ; Captain Monroe of the Board of Trade was also present.

The promoters were represented by two solicitors, the fishing by Mr. Cowlard, clerk to the County Council. I had previously furnished Mr. Cowlard with the following agenda, and was prepared to call witnesses against the scheme, one of the most valuable and important being the late Sir Edward Hain.

In opening the case for the promotors, one of the solicitors said that his remarks with reference to tin in St. Ives Bay would stagger us, and he made the statement in all sobriety, that at the present time there was in the Bay from £20,000,000 worth of tin, to a figure which it would be impossible to name.

It was pointed out that the portion of the Bay scheduled was the best herring part ; however, at the conclusion of the enquiry, the inspectors saw for themselves the fishing fleet, as usual, making direct for the fishing ground, and at night the lights on the boats drifting over the very ground asked for. Shortly after a similar application was made for permission to dredge for tin in Bassett's Bay, the same objection was raised, and this also was frustrated.

I never could ascertain how the £20,000,000 was arrived at ; there is no doubt a certain amount of tin does escape, but the soundings are the same.

DREDGING FOR TIN IN ST. IVES BAY

" At the Conference to be held at the Council Chamber on Friday the 12th inst., Colonel Williams will open on behalf of the Fishermen, and will present, as follows, viz. :—

(1) Chart of St. Ives Bay, showing the portion scheduled by the Promoters.

(2) Copy of Resolution passed by the Cornwall Fisheries Com.

(3) Ditto, ditto Seine Owners.

(4) Ditto, ditto at the Public Meeting of Fishermen held at St. Ives on April 19th, 1913.

(5) The Pilchard Fishery Act.

(6) Copy of the Promoters' application to the Board of Trade. ———

(1) That there are at St. Ives from 400 to 500 men engaged in the fishing industry.

(2) That 240 of them are Royal Naval Reserve Men ready to be called out when required, and 125 of them are in possession of long service medals.

(3) That from time immemorial St. Ives fisher-

men have had undisputed fishing all over the Bay.

(4) That the Herring Fishing has been, and is of considerable value and importance not only to the fishermen but also to the town.

(5) That the largest quantity is caught at the eastern side of the bay in the portion scheduled by the promoters.

(6) That in the eight years from 1904 to 1911 herrings of the value of £91,000 were caught on the eastern side.

(7) That at present there are 85 boats engaged in herring fishing.

(8) That it is well known that the shoals of herrings and pilchards enter the bay from the north through Godrevy Sound."

In connection with the fishing industry, and also with the mercantile marine, there are two points of interest I should also mention, they are :

(1) A better fog apparatus at Godrevy Lighthouse.

(2) Communication between Lighthouses and Lightships and the main land.

As regards the first, I had considerable correspondence and many interviews with the authorities at Trinity House, and I now insert copies of correspondence in connection therewith and also with the Board of Trade, which give particulars of my action and the result.

(*Copy*)   TRINITY HOUSE, LONDON, E.C.
15*th December*, 1905.

SIR,

Your further letter on the subject of the fog signal at Godrevy Light House has been under consideration, and I am now directed to inform you that the Elder Brethren are of opinion that any more expensive form of signal than that at this particular station is not required, seeing buoy in a position about one and a half miles from the Light House, which, with the bell, should be sufficient to warn vessels of their position.

I am to add that, if any additional signal is required for vessels entering St. Ives Harbour, the Elder Brethren think it should be provided by the Local Authorities at that place.

Yours truly,
(Signed)   A. OWEN.

ST. IVES, CORNWALL,
January 17th, 1906.

SIR,   Godrevy Light House.

I cannot but think your letter of the 15th ulto. was written under a misapprehension, for if you take the Admiralty chart of that part of the coast, it will be seen that between the reef of rocks (known as the Stones) and the lighthouse there is a deep-water channel, known as the Sound, and this is the course taken by vessels trading to and from the Bristol Channel, Hayle and St. Ives, and the whistling buoy one and a half miles away is of little advantage to those taking the Sound channel, and the fishermen and pilots say that if the bell is heard at all it is not more than a tinkle.

(Signed)   H. W. WILLIAMS.

As to communication between Light Houses and Lightships :—

BOARD OF TRADE, LONDON,
June 16th, 1915.

DEAR COLONEL WILLIAMS,

In reply to your letter of the 31st May last, respecting the suggested establishment of wireless telegraphic communication between the Longships and Wolf Rock Light Houses, I have to inform you, that it has been reported to the Board that three aerial wires installed at the latter Light House were broken by heavy seas during a gale on the 1st of January last, and that the Corporation of Trinity House do not propose to conduct any experiments during the period of the War with a view of establishing Wireless Telegraphy at that Light House.

Faithfully yours,
(Signed)   GARNHAM ROPER.

*   *   *

In concluding these imperfect memories, I cannot altogether ignore this terrible war, which we must all earnestly hope will soon terminate ; my references to it will, however, be very brief.

In addition to my other public duties, I have for over two years been sitting as a member of the Cornwall County Tribunal. At some of the meetings painful cases have arisen, yet I am satisfied the Tribunal has faithfully endeavoured to do its duty impartially.

I have previously stated that in 1856 I saw the Guards on their arrival in London after the Crimean victories ; I now look forward to an early date to see our victorious Army return to England, and I am certain they will receive, as the Crimean Guards did, a magnificent reception.

From *The Times*, April 17th, 1918 :—
"Lieutenant-Colonel Henry Willey Williams is gazetted Deputy-Lieutenant for Cornwall."